THE GIRL IN THE MIRROR

R. E. Collins

PublishAmerica
Baltimore

© 2014 by R. E. Collins.
All rights reserved. No part of this book may be reproduced, stored in a retrieval system or transmitted in any form or by any means without the prior written permission of the publishers, except by a reviewer who may quote brief passages in a review to be printed in a newspaper, magazine or journal.

First printing

All characters in this book are fictitious, and any resemblance to real persons, living or dead, is coincidental.

PublishAmerica has allowed this work to remain exactly as the author intended, verbatim, without editorial input.

Softcover 9781630841836
PUBLISHED BY PUBLISHAMERICA, LLLP
www.publishamerica.com
Baltimore

Printed in the United States of America

Dedications

Dedicated to my loving wife, Tasha, my daughters: Brooke and Janna, my God-kids: Ryen, Cadie and Jill and their mother Christy and to all my friends who helped bring my dream of writing a book come true.

Acknowledgements

I would like to thank a very special, drama teacher and dear friend of mine, John Wheeler, for all of his encouraging words, early morning and late night talks, and belief in me. Especially for the words, "Dream Big, Believe, and Achieve."

Prologue: A Dad's Heartbreak

He ended his day like every other day. Well almost every other day. Today he decided that he would stop by the local pub on his way home from work. His best friend, Jerry, had been after him for weeks now to stop in and have a few beers and to shoot a few games of pool. So today he gave in. Before he went in, he called his daughter. ***"Hey you've reached Melanie; you know what to do," was the answer he received, from the other end of the line.*** He left a message and went inside. Jerry was at the bar waiting for him when he got there. "What are you having Mac," Jerry asked? "I'll have an ice cold beer," He replied. Jerry ordered two beers and asked the bartender, for ten dollars' worth of quarters. Once he got the beers and change they headed for the tables. Before Mac knew it, time had completely slipped away from him. He was well on his way to becoming shitfaced. Suddenly, he realized that he still had about a thirty minute drive, down I-10, before he made it home, so he decided to call it a night. "Are you sure you have to go" Jerry asked. "I am sure" Mac replied. "We will definitely do this again, I promise," He said as he headed out the door. He knew better than to drive under the influence but he had to get home to Melanie. He jumped into his '96 Glossy Black, Chevy Tahoe, fired the engine up and headed home. Mac was being extra cautious, so it took him close to an hour to get there. When he pulled into the driveway he noticed that Mel's '85 canary yellow Camaro was in its usual parking spot. He glanced at his watch and because time had gotten away from him, he decided to slip into the house and go directly upstairs, to the bathroom, to get cleaned up. After a long, hot, and steamy shower, he went straight to bed. Awakened by the sound of thunder, he noticed the alarm clock sitting on the bedside table. Hmmm, he thought to himself, it is four fifteen in the morning. Mac checked his phone and saw that he had three missed calls and a voicemail. "Damn! I must have been dead to the world," He said. He opened his phone and saw that the missed calls had all been from Melanie. So, he immediately got worried. He dialed his voicemail and listened to the message. *"Hi Dad, sorry I missed your call last night. Did you forget that Tamara and I were going to a concert? We did not get back until late, so I crashed at her house. I love you, see you in the morning. Oh and dad, I need to talk to you, it's important."* After listening to the message, his mind was a little more at ease. He got up, pissed, and then decided that he would try to get a few more hours of sleep. He closed his eyes but could not help to wonder, what it was that she wanted to talk to him about. He tossed and turned for several more hours and since he couldn't sleep; he decided that he would get up and straighten the house, while he waited. The phone rang. He picked it up, looked at the caller ID and saw that it was his friend Jerry on the other end. He reluctantly answered it. "Hey Mac, it is a perfect day to go fishing. Let's go hit up Wild Bill's pond!" "Let me holler back at you in a little while Jerry, Mel wants to talk to me and she says it's important." Mac hung up the phone, moved the curtain to the side and looked out the window. He was just about to walk away, when he saw Tamara's car pulling into the drive. He walked back over to the couch and waited for his daughter to come inside. He hoped he could handle it, whatever "it" was. She came in and threw her stuff onto the counter, then walked over to the couch where he was sitting. Mac could tell by the look on his daughters' face that something was wrong. Tears began to form in her eyes as she took her daddy's hand. Then it was as is if someone had turned on a water faucet, because the tears began running nonstop down her cheeks. She looked up at her daddy and said in almost a whisper, "I miss her dad, I miss mom." Her mother had been diagnosed with stage IV breast cancer shortly after giving birth and died when Melanie was just five years old. The doctors said it wasn't the cancer that got her but it was the major complications that came along with it, that ultimately took her life. Mac held his daughter without saying a word, for what seemed like hours but in reality it was just for a few seconds, then he finally said, "I do to Mel, but what is really bothering you? I have always been there for you and have always stood behind you no matter what and that will never change." She looked up into her daddy's eyes and said, "Dad I really messed up this time. I've let you down many times in the last seventeen years but this time, I have really messed up." "Mel, I will not pretend that I have always agreed with the things you have done but one thing you have never been to me is a disappointment. Just tell me how you think you messed up." "Dad I don't think, I know. I went to the health department yesterday before going to the concert. I'm pregnant!" Mac lost all color in his face and he became extremely quiet. Melanie just sat there with her head in her hands crying uncontrollably. Then all at once, Mac spoke in a tone of voice Mel had never heard and will not soon forget. "Who is the father? I will kill the son of a bitch." She had never seen her father so upset and really did not know what to say. She had just single handedly ripped her dad's heart out. Because of the circumstances surrounding her pregnancy, she knew she had to do the unimaginable. Something she had never ever done before. Melanie was going to have to lie to her dad and that is exactly what she did. She told her dad that she went to a party, where she started playing beer pong and that she had passed out. When she had awoke the next morning, she was completely naked. So, that's when she assumed, that she had been drugged and taken advantage of. "Did you call the police or go to the hospital?" "Yes dad, but I felt so dirty, so I took a shower. The police said that they couldn't do anything, because there was no evidence showing that anything had taken place. Dad, I am so sorry but I am going to take care of this." "How are you going to take care of it? Your seventeen years old for Christ's sake. You will not have an abortion; you know my thoughts on that." "I know dad, but I cannot take care of them either." "What do you mean them?" "Dad, I am not just pregnant, I am pregnant with twins." After hearing that, the tears began to trickle down his cheeks and he became extremely silent for the second time in just a matter of a minutes. He got up and walked to the kitchen. "Dad, please do not shut me out." Mac turned and looked at his daughter and calmly said, "Mel, I love you to the moon and back, but this is your mess so you damn well better fix it." "I will dad; I am going to give them up for adoption." "Well, I think I am going to go fishing with Jerry and it may be late when I get home." Mac walked over to his daughter and hugged her without saying another word. He kissed the top of her head, like he had done every day since she had been born, then walked out the door. Melanie sat there on the couch, crying her eyes out for many reasons. (She had gone to a party, she had gotten drunk, she had had sexual intercourse (multiple times) and enjoyed it, she had gotten pregnant, but worst of all she had bold face lied to her father. After wallowing in self-pity, she decided to visit her mom's grave). By the time she pulled into the first entrance of Memorial Gardens, Melanie had stopped crying. She got out of the car and walked a short distance along a concrete walkway, up to a big old oak tree, which was standing so tall, right in the center of the cemetery.

Next to the base of that mighty oak laid a tombstone. On the tombstone was inscribed these words: "Margaret Coleman, Devoted Wife-Beloved Mother." Melanie laid on the ground atop of her mother's grave, as if her head were lying on her mother's shoulder and the tears started to flow yet again. "Oh mom, it has been such a long time since I've come by to talk to you but I need your advice now more than ever. I've really messed up and I don't know if things will ever be the same. Mom I have messed around and have gotten myself pregnant with twins. I guess, I am living proof of the old saying "if you play you pay." Mom in the letter you left for me before you died, you told me that "no one could help who they fell in love with" and you could not have been more right. I fell in love with Pastor Ellis's son, Bobby. He is ten years my senior but you also told me, in your letter, that age was just a number. Dad doesn't like Bobby. Dad called him a stalker because he caught him flirting with me, when I used to ride the school bus he drove. I had to lie to dad because when he questioned me about the father of my babies, he said, "he would kill the son of a bitch". I am going to give the babies up for adoption. I know that giving them to someone who could raise them in a stable environment is the right thing to do but why does it hurt like hell? It wasn't supposed to happen this way. I was supposed to fall in love and be proposed to. Mom, you were supposed to help me with my wedding dress, my hair and my make-up. Dad was supposed to walk me down the aisle. Then, I was supposed to have a honeymoon and live a little before getting pregnant. Oh Mom! Why did it not happen like that?" Melanie laid there on her mother's grave until dusk was just beginning to set in. She got up and looked back at the tombstone and as she read the words "Beloved Mother" a smile came across her face. She whispered, "Thanks mom you are the best." She realized then and there what she had to do, to fix things between her and her dad. She was going to do what she was always taught to do, by her parents. Melanie was going to tell the truth, not just part of it but the whole truth. She pulled back up at home and noticed her dad still had not made it back. She decided to take a hot relaxing bubble bath and then she would fix her dad's favorite meal, homemade lasagna, for supper. She had just gotten the table set, when she heard her dad's Tahoe pull into the drive. He walked in and the aroma of fresh baked garlic bread and the scent of lasagna hit him and he immediately began to smile. His smile only lasted until he looked at the table and he saw five place settings. His eyes shot directly to his daughter and she spoke ever so softly. "Pastor Ellis, his wife Brooke, and their son Bobby will be joining us for dinner. Dad, you told me to fix this mess so trust me. After tonight you will know everything and you will see that things will work out. I need us to be the way we were dad. The way we were before I had the talk with you this morning. The Ellis's will be here at seven thirty. Go get cleaned up, you have thirty minutes and you smell of chicken livers and beer." Mac gave a little chuckle and walked up the stairs. As Melanie was waiting on her company to arrive, she had a million emotions running through her mind. However, she knew that the purpose for tonight was for one reason and one reason only. She had to repair the damage that she had caused between her and her dad. Even if it hurt everyone else involved. Mac was on his way down the stairs, just as he heard the doorbell ring. He opened the door and invited the Ellis's into his home. Melanie took a deep breath and pulled herself together the best she could. She finished placing the lasagna, garlic bread, and salad onto the table and then she took a seat. "Pastor Ellis, if you would be so kind as to say grace," said Mac. "Melanie this looks and smells great, Brooke said." "Thank you Mrs. Ellis" She replied. Everyone began eating but at the same time everyone could feel the tension in the air. It was Pastor Ellis that first broke the silence. "Melanie, it has been awhile since I have seen you in a service. Is everything alright?" Mac shot a look her way and then looked back down at his plate. "Well, Pastor Ellis, the truth is, I actually have something I need to tell you and Mrs. Ellis." "Well you know what they say, confessions are good for the soul," He replied. "Well that remains to be seen," Mel replied. She took a deep breath and then without holding anything back she began "confessing." "Mr. and Mrs. Ellis, for the better part of this year, Bobby and I have been seeing each other. A couple months ago, I accompanied him to a party. At this party, we drank and eventually became intimate. We had unprotected sex several times, throughout the night and as fate would have it, I got pregnant. I am not just pregnant but I am pregnant with twins. Before you all think bad of me, I am giving the babies up for adoption. I am just seventeen and I cannot raise these kids on my own. I also cannot commit to a relationship with Bobby at this time in my life either. We may say we love each other now but I have to pursue my dreams. I am definitely way too young to settle down and start a family. I have contacted the Texas Department of Family and Protective Services and have told them of my decision. Bobby, it's not really necessary but things will go a lot smoother, if you sign over your parental rights. I apologize for dumping this on all of you like this but it was the only way I knew to do it. I am sorry Bobby, I love you but as of now, I am ending our relationship. Pastor Ellis, I regret this entire turn of events but under the circumstances I will not be returning to the church or at least not until after the babies have been born. Mrs. Ellis, I do not know what to say to you. You and mom were so close. I know I have let everyone involved down and all I can do is apologize. Dad I realize it's going to take you a while to process all of this but I hope one day you can forgive me. I am going to excuse myself; I hope you all have a great night. Sorry if I ruined dinner." After Mac let his houseguests out, he went to the fridge and grabbed a beer, then, he sat down in his recliner. He sat there trying to grasp what the hell had just happened. After about an hour had past, Mac heard Melanie cleaning up from supper. He got up out of his recliner and finished helping his daughter with the dishes. When they had finally cleaned up, they looked at each other and without either of them saying a word; Melanie started to cry, so Mac grabbed his daughter and stood there in the kitchen hugging her tightly. She finally whispered the words, "dad I am scared, please tell me everything is going to be alright." "As long as the Sun rises in the morning and the Moon and Stars light up the night skies, my love shall surround you and shall keep you safe from all that abounds." Those words that came out of his mouth caught her by surprise because she hadn't heard them since she was ten. "Mel, I cannot pretend like none of this has happened but I can promise that I will try to understand it and I will do my best to be here for you and the babies until they are born." "That is all I ever wanted dad, I just want you to be there for me like you have always been." She kisses his cheek and goes to bed. Mac goes to the kitchen, opens up the fridge and decides to pop the top on one more cold beer before heading up the stairs and calling it a night himself.

Part One: The Accident

Chapter 1

The next few months flew by fast. With help from the school's guidance counselor, Melanie managed to finish all of her classes early, ensuring she would graduate. The babies' due date was estimated to be two days before graduation, so she was not planning on walking with her class. Instead, she had arranged to receive her diploma by mail. Mac kept his promise to support his daughter and to be there for her. Things were not a hundred percent like they once were but they were getting there. Mac and his daughter spent almost every night after dinner, catching up on old re-runs of one of television's most popular crime drama's and asking each other about their day. Tonight was no exception. Mac could always tell when something was bothering his daughter. "What's wrong?" "Tomorrow I go for my eight month check-up," She replied. "Do you want me to call in to work and go with you?" "No dad, you don't have to do that. I am just nervous that's all." "You'll be fine. I may stop by the pub and meet Jerry after work but call me when you get out of the doctor's office and I will meet you back here and maybe if you're feeling up to it, I will take you out to your favorite restaurant for dinner." "Sounds great dad, I love you." "I love you too Mel, goodnight." "Goodnight dad."

Chapter 2

Mel had her alarm clock set for eight thirty a.m. but it wasn't the alarm that woke her up. She was awakened by a rolling clap of thunder. She got out of bed and made her way to the bathroom, where she preceded to run a tub full of bath water. Her appointment wasn't until three o'clock in the afternoon, so she thought she might stop in at the nail salon before tackling the short thirty minute drive to her appointment. As she was laying in the bath soaking she began to feel a little queasy. It was not morning sickness because that had passed months ago. She laid there for a few more minutes and decided to get out and dry off. The queasiness eventually subsided but then she began to experience sever cramping. It wasn't contractions or at least she didn't think it was. She found a matching bra and panty set and put them on, then stretched out across her bed. After lying there for a few minutes her cramping also eased up. So, she finished getting ready and headed out the door. Mel stopped by the salon and got her nails done and then looked down at her watch and realized time was really starting to fly by. The traffic on I-10 was unusually heavy and with the storm fast approaching, she knew she would be pushing it to make it on time. She pulled into the clinic's lot with just five minutes to spare.

Chapter 3

"Miss Coleman, come on back." Melanie stepped up on the scales and couldn't believe she had gained another five pounds since her last visit. Miss Coleman have you experienced any kind of cramping or nausea since your last appointment?" "Yes ma'am, I felt queasy and had cramps this morning." "Have you experienced any noticeable amount of swelling?" "No ma'am not that I am aware of." "One more question, Miss Coleman, have the babies still been fairly active?" "Actually, I haven't felt them as much lately but yes, they still move around." "Okay, let me take your blood pressure and get a urine sample, then the doctor will be in momentarily." After about twenty minutes had passed the doctor finally came in and introduced himself. "Hi, I'm Dr. Matthews and I just got off the phone with your regular physician and it seems he agrees with me about the next steps, we should take." "What do you mean next steps?" "Well Miss Coleman, your blood pressure is a wee bit on the high side, we are also a little concerned with the level of protein in your urine, add that to the decrease in baby movement, and the nausea and cramping that you have been experiencing and the fact that your ankles seem to be swelling. We believe that you are showing sure signs of preeclampsia." "So, what are the "next steps" you were referring to," She asked, in a concerned voice. "Well honestly, what we need for you to do is to go home and pack a bag. We are going to have to deliver these babies Miss Coleman." She nodded towards the doctor, acknowledging what he was saying but at the same time, she was trying to hold it together. She was scared to death and all she wanted was her daddy. Melanie had just gotten into her car and shut the door when the bottom fell out. The rain was falling so hard she could barely see five feet in front of her. She just sat there in the car recalling the words of Dr. Matthews, "We are going to have to get those babies out!" She dialed her dads' number while she waited and prayed for the rain to slack off. She let it ring twice and then hung up. Melanie and her dad used the two ring method as a way of letting each other know there was something wrong. Mac called her right back. "What's wrong, Mel?" "Dad, they are admitting me into the hospital tonight and they are going to induce labor. The doctors believe I have preeclampsia but are allowing me time to go home and pack a bag." "Baby everything will be fine. I will meet you at the house and then I will take you back to the hospital. We should get home about the same time. Oh and honey be careful it's really getting bad out there. You will be driving right into this mess." "Ok, I will dad. I am already buckled in, so I'm going to get off here and head your way." Melanie pulled out of the parking lot and took a right on the ramp leading to the I-10. Her dad told her that she would be driving into the storm but she didn't realize just how bad it would be. Of course, as fate would have it, not only was she driving into the approaching storm, she had gotten herself caught up in rush hour traffic. People didn't seem to care that it was storming; they just wanted to get home after a hard day's work. They were weaving back and forth from lane to lane, trying to find a quicker way to get where they were going. Melanie decided to maintain sixty miles per hour and to stay in the outside lane because she knew that she would have to take the Geronimo Drive exit, which was exit 24. She had just passed Mesa Street which was exit 19A. The rain was relentless. It seemed the farther she drove, the more visibility decreased. There were an unusual amount of "Big Rigs" as they were often called, on the I-10 for this time of day, Mel thought to herself. They usually got on after rush hour, to make runs back and forth across the Louisiana State line, hauling cargo of different sorts. It wasn't long until Melanie found herself surrounded by three tractor trailers. One was in front, one in back, and one to her immediate left. She became extremely nervous. She kept thinking that her exit should be coming up, but she didn't like her predicament. She decided to slow down a little and when she did the rig beside her sped up and decided to swap lanes. I am not sure whether the driver of the rig lost sight of the Canary Yellow Camaro that was beside him because of the blind spot between his truck and trailer or if something distracted him, but as he swapped lanes he forced Melanie off of the road. Her car spun out of control, then crossed the median and was struck head on by a Glossy Black Tahoe.

Part Two: The Aftermath

Chapter 4

It wasn't long before rush hour traffic became a traffic nightmare. People were getting out of their cars and running to the rescue but soon realizing there was nothing that anyone could do. Sirens began to wail in the distance, signaling that emergency help was on the way. Once emergency personnel arrived on scene it looked like something out of a horror film. They worked fast and efficiently to get the patients out of their vehicles. To onlookers, it didn't seem like anyone should have survived this horrific accident because there was blood everywhere. Paramedics worked with both patients; however, neither patient was conscious. Both patients had severe head trauma and both patients were in critical condition. The female victim however, was the most important at the moment. One of the paramedics realized that she was pregnant and they knew that they had at least three patients to save now instead of just two. As the ambulances left the scene people began to scatter and scurry back to their awaiting cars. They hoped that the mess left behind by this disastrous collision would be cleaned up and traffic would begin to flow again, so that they could get home to their loved ones. It wasn't until the patients were admitted into the emergency room that their identities were revealed. Identification was taken from the female patients' purse, which identified her as seventeen year old Melanie Coleman and the driver's license recovered from John Doe's wallet identified him as Mac Coleman. Upon further investigation it was determined that the two victims involved in the accident on I-10 were father and daughter.

News spread fast throughout the hospital among the nurses and staff. Eventually word reached the chapel. Pastor Ellis had been at the hospital that evening praying with the family of one of his elder members. He heard that a father and daughter had been rushed in and that their outcomes were not looking great. So he decided to go see if he could pray over them. He was told that the female was in the operating room having a C-section but that her father was in ICU room 1104. He scrubbed up and entered the room. He took two steps into the room and realized that the person lying in the hospital bed in front of him, hooked up to all those tubes, was Mac. Then it hit him. Melanie is having a C-section and she is all alone. So Pastor Ellis said a prayer over Mac and then he called his wife and son. Even though Melanie and Bobby weren't together anymore they did still talk as friends. Bobby was with his mother so it did not take long for them to join Pastor Ellis at the hospital. They were the closest thing to family, other than Mac, that Mel had at the time. So they all gathered in the waiting room, hoping that they would receive word, on what was going on. It seemed like an eternity before that word came but finally it did. "Is there someone here with the Coleman family," asked the receptionist? Pastor Ellis got to the desk and after explaining the situation to the receptionist she handed the phone to him. "This is Dr. Long; we were able to deliver both babies by caesarian section, however, Miss Coleman began losing a lot of blood. We tried to find the cause of the bleeding, which we did. However, before getting the bleeding to stop her blood pressure began to drop dangerously low. She then went into cardiac arrest. We tried to resuscitate her for five minutes to no avail. We called time of death at 17:50. The cause of death will be accredited to injuries sustained during a motor vehicle accident. Are there any questions you would like to ask?" "What will happen to the babies," Pastor Ellis asked? "As per the request of the now deceased, babies John and Jane Doe will be checked over and after they are given a clean bill of health, the Texas Department of Family and Protective Services will be notified. So when they are discharged tomorrow the TDF&P will be solely responsible for their well-being. Again I am sorry for you loss, goodbye." Pastor Ellis handed the receptionist back the phone but it took him a few minutes before he turned around. He was trying to gather his composure before he broke the news. When he returned to his wife and son he told them that the babies were fine. Bobby immediately asked about Melanie. When his brown eyes made contact with his father's he knew the answer. He screamed the words; ***"all of this is my fault, I killed her"*** before running out of the hospital.

Chapter 5

Pastor Ellis knew that Mac had a sister that he didn't talk to on a regular basis, but it was all the family he had left, now that Mel was gone. It took him about twenty four hours to locate her and fill her in. She agreed to come down and make funeral arrangements for her niece. She kept the services as simple as she could. After a short visitation by Tamara and the rest of her friends, they had a small grave side service underneath that big old oak tree. Melanie Anne Coleman was laid to rest, as if, "her head were lying on her mother's shoulder." Two more weeks would pass before the swelling in Mac's brain decreased enough for him to begin to come out of his coma. He opened his eyes to find a room full of people. He scanned the room two or three times before he spoke. Then he said with a panicked voice, "Where is Mel?" No one answered, so he asked again. Still no one answered. This time he screamed, "Where is my daughter?" Then reality hit him like a ton of bricks. Everyone, I am fine! He exclaimed. "Now, everyone can get the hell out of my room, except for Pastor Ellis." Once everybody left his room he looked into the Pastor's eyes and said, "Tell that no good son of yours, he is to blame for my daughter's death and when I get out of here, I'm going to kill him!" "I would be glad to tell him if I could find him, but he hasn't been seen since the day she died. Your sister, Mary, has not left your side since you've been here. Jerry has been by several times as well, but he said you knew how he felt about hospitals. I'm sorry for your loss. Mac this is going to take time. If you need anything, call me." Once Mac was sure he was alone he cried. The two most important women in his life were together again and he was lying in a hospital bed wondering why. "Why not take my life instead," ran through his mind continuously? He was discharged two days after waking up. His first stop was to the hospital flower shop. He bought two dozen red roses for his two favorite ladies, and then he went to see them in the cemetery. He decided he couldn't live in the house he once shared with his beloved wife and daughter so he moved in with his sister Mary. He frequently visits his best pal Jerry and just as often takes that walk down the concrete walkway that leads to that great big mighty oak. At the base of that oak tree there are two tombstones. One is inscribed: "Margaret Coleman, Devoted Wife-Beloved Mother" the other is inscribed: "Melanie Anne Coleman, Momma's Angel-Daddy's Little Girl."

Part Three: New Beginnings

Chapter 6

Jane and John Doe were released from the hospital into the custody of the Texas Department of Family and Protective Services as expected. The TDF&P services already had two families waiting to adopt the children. This particular adoption was set-up as a closed adoption, meaning that all background information surrounding the birth mother/father and the child/children being given up would remain sealed and the only person allowed to view the sealed information would be the children's case worker. The children were assigned to Miss Elizabeth Evans. Miss Evans was a young, very attractive woman with a heart of gold. She would be the person entrusted to make sure that the infants are placed with their proper families and subsequently, also be responsible for making sure the children adjust to their new environments by conducting their yearly follow-ups. After all her I's were dotted and all her Tee's were crossed, Miss Evans was ready to proceed with her top two priority cases. She picked up the folder marked Jane and John Doe and after thumbing through the pages, she found what she was looking for. She picked up the phone and dialed the number for Mr. and Mrs. Hall. The phone began ringing and then after the third ring, a woman on the other end answered. "Hello." "Yes this is Elizabeth Evans and I am with the TDF&P. Is this Mrs. Hall?" "Yes but please call me Renee." "Okay Renee, I am calling to let you know that the baby you and your husband are adopting was born a few days ago." "No, that can't be. We have another month before she is due. My husband is still working on the nursery in our new house, in Tennessee." "Ma'am, I'm sorry, she is here but don't worry, everything is fine. When do you think that you both could come in to finalize everything?" "He will be back tomorrow." "Great, Mrs. Hall, I will see you tomorrow." After hanging up the phone, Renee began to realize her dream of becoming a mother was becoming a reality. Her husband, who was a truck driver, decided that he wanted to do everything he could to support his wife's dream. He put in a month's notice with his Trucking Company and also applied for a supervisor position at a factory in Nashville, Tennessee. Even before hearing from the factory, Martin took a leap of faith and bought a house out in the country about ten miles away from his potential new place of employment. The house was set on five acres of land and had four bedrooms and two and a half baths. It was really his and his wife's dream home, complete with everything, including a white picket fence. It was the perfect place to raise a family. He had decided to take one of the bedrooms and turn it into a nursery. He had been working on it in his spare time and hoped that he would have it done by the time him and Renee brought Katrina home. Yes, they had decided to name Baby Jane Doe, Katrina.

Chapter 7

It was mid-morning, when Martin and Renee, decided to make the short trip across town to meet with Miss Evans. They both had butterflies in their stomachs as they entered the building. They knew that when they left, they would be parents of a newborn baby girl. They asked the receptionist at the door where they could find Elizabeth Evans, and they were instructed to take the elevator to the 2nd floor where Miss Evans would meet them. As the elevator doors opened and they stepped out, they saw a woman standing with her back to them. She was holding something in her arms. As they reached the woman standing there, they could see a newborn baby wrapped in a pink receiving blanket. Then reality hit them. Miss Evans turned, smiled, and then handed Renee their baby girl, and said, "Congratulations you are now a mother." Tears began to well up in her eyes as she realized her dream had just come true. After Mr. and Mrs. Hall finished signing all the documents and listening to every detail and obligation they were now charged with, they were dismissed. Miss Evans couldn't help but feel a heart-warming sensation, deep down in her soul, as she watched the new family leave her office.

Chapter 8

She went back to her desk and picked up the file she had thumbed through just one day earlier. She again flipped through the pages until she found the number for Mr. and Mrs. Jacks. She dialed the number and the phone rang just twice, before a voice on the other end answered. It had been the housekeeper that picked up. Elizabeth explained who she was and the housekeeper informed her that Richard and Marianne Jacks were both surgeons at Texas Memorial Hospital and that they were both in surgery but that they would both be home tomorrow. Elizabeth left her number and told the housekeeper to make sure Mr. and Mrs. Jacks got in touch with her as soon as possible. Early the next morning, the Jacks' called and made arrangements to meet Miss Evans in order to finalize their adoption of Baby John Doe. After all arrangements were made and finalized Richard and Marianne Jacks took home their newborn son, Jeffrey. After both babies had been placed with their families, Elizabeth breathed a huge sigh of relief. However, she knew this was just the beginning of a very long process. She knew that she would play a minor part in the lives of these kids for at least the next eighteen years.

Chapter 9

Time began flying by. It had been five years since the death of Melanie and the adoption of her twins, Katrina Hall and Jeffrey Jacks. Their adoptive parents had kept in touch with their respective Departments of Family and Protective Services once per year as instructed. Over the past five years each child had been physically progressing right on schedule as other kids their age but mentally was a different story. Katrina or Kat for short was reportedly progressing ahead of kids her age. She was reading on a 2nd grade level. Jeffrey or" J.J." for short was also reportedly ahead of kids his age. His memory skills were off the chart and he was on a 3rd grade math level but he was also reportedly very distant. He didn't talk very much at all and when he did, it was to himself. He played with toys but he didn't play with them as they were intended to be played with. His mother and father didn't really think it was anything to worry about at the moment but the nanny was concerned. Elizabeth agreed with the Jacks' nanny. She decided that since Katrina lived in Tennessee now and she seemed to be progressing very well that she would concentrate solely on Jeffrey and closely monitor his growth in the coming months. She didn't like the fact he was distant, didn't communicate to a physical person efficiently and didn't play with toys like he should. Her immediate thought was that J.J. may be experiencing early signs of Autism, but that wasn't for her to decide. After monitoring his growth for a while if she decided he needed an evaluation, she would consult with his parents and recommend a specialist to do just that. Elizabeth made plans to spend a few hours with J.J. every Friday afternoon.

The Jacks' spent most Fridays at the hospital, leaving J.J. with his nanny. Elizabeth met with the nanny and explained to her that she wanted her to go through her normal routine and that she would just sit back and jot down a few notes. After the first few visits, Miss Evans realized that the nanny's' concerns were definitely justifiable. She called Dr. Shaw, who was the most respected Autism specialist in the state of Texas. He agreed to have J.J. brought in for a few tests. It would be a few weeks before Dr. Shaw could see him. The night before he was to be brought in something happened that scared everyone. He was instructed by the nanny to go brush his teeth and to get ready for bed. The nanny was in his room getting his bed ready when she heard glass breaking. She ran to the bathroom to find J.J. sitting beside the tub, white as a ghost, and shaking uncontrollably. There was a drinking glass broke in the sink. The nanny asked him what happened. "She scared me." "Who scared you?" "The girl, the girl in the mirror, she scared me and I dropped my glass of water. Is she still there?" "I don't see anything but my own reflection, she replied." He slowly got up and looked into the mirror and he too only saw his own reflection. "Can you stay with me until I fall asleep, Noni?" He asked. "Yes J.J., I will stay with you," she replied.

Chapter 10

The next morning the nanny filled in Mr. and Mrs. Jacks about the incident that had occurred. Although it was troubling, they decided not to ask J.J. about it, instead they would leave it up to the doctor to inquire. They arrived at the office of Dr. Shaw and then reality began to set in, the reality that they spend so much time at the hospital; they miss out on a lot of their sons' firsts. They also started realizing for the first time, that maybe they did miss something and that something was wrong with their son. Once inside the office they signed in and were instructed by the young woman behind the counter to take a seat, and that they would be called back as quickly as possible. When Dr. Shaw was ready, he came out and talked to the Jacks. He explained to them he wanted to conduct the tests alone and then he would consult with them when it was over. However, J.J. wasn't having it. He was being clingy this morning, so Dr. Shaw allowed his mother to come back with him. After a series of tests and questions, Dr. Shaw had the answer he was looking for; however, he wanted one more person to talk to J.J. before he discussed things over with his parents. He called in Dr. Conner, a child psychiatrist. Dr. Conner heard about the incident involving the mirror and the reflection that J.J. had seen and after discussing it with him, he determined that his pre-diagnosis was correct or at least he believed it to be. The Doctors conferred with each other and then called the Jack's into the conference room to discuss their findings. Once in the conference room Dr. Shaw introduced Dr. Conner then he began to speak openly to Richard and

Marianne about their son. "Well I have good news. Your son is not Autistic. When I spoke to him he made eye contact. When I asked him to repeat after me, he repeated everything back to me clearly. He also separated the toys I laid down by colors just as I instructed. I asked him why he didn't talk much at home and he said he just felt lonely because his parents never played with him. He isn't talking to himself; he has an imaginary friend named Teddy that he talks to. Research shows that it is normal for kids to have imaginary friends because it shows that they have a creative side. Usually these "friends" fade away as the child matures and starts interacting with more and more kids. Now the other area I was concerned with was the incident that happened last night. That's where Dr. Conner comes in." "Now, what I wanted to do was to ask J.J. about what happened and I wanted to listen to him. Once he got to the part about looking into the mirror he visibly started shaking and his heart rate began to climb. Mr. and Mrs. Jacks, I believe your son is suffering from Eisoptrophobia or Spectrophobia. In English, that means your son is afraid of mirrors and/or his own reflection. Once he starts shaking and his heart rate goes up his mind starts over working and he sees things that are not there. There are a few things we can do to try and help, but I believe he will eventually grow out of this." Marianne spoke up and asked, "What could have caused this?" "Well, it is hard to say but according to studies a child may have been traumatized, where they believed they may have heard or seen ghosts or scary images in the mirror. Some younger kids become scared if they have seen horror movies in which things actually came out of mirrors." "What can we do to help him," asked Richard? "Well aside from medication and/or certain therapeutic measures, we can only hope he grows out of it. Worst case scenario he will begin to see things that are not there in anything that may cast a reflection." "We appreciate you taking a look at him and for all the information but this is a lot to take in. His mother and I will take him home and we will schedule a follow up with you next week. Can you call Miss Evans and let her know about the diagnosis." "Not a problem, Mr. Jacks, not a problem." After taking their son home, the Jacks' realized they had a decision to make. They could put their five year old son on medication and put him through therapy or they could see if he out grew these phobias. As doctors they knew how hard it was for toddlers to be put on medication. So, after a very short discussion, they decided to call Dr. Conner back and let him know that they had opted for no medication or therapy. That decision proved to be a bad choice.

Chapter 11

For the next twelve years, at least twice a week, he was graced with the appearance of an unknown reflection and not just in passing a mirror. The strange thing was the older he got, the older the "girl in the mirror" got. He had just about gotten used to the fact that he would see this reflection from time to time and he was just about to the point that it didn't really bother him anymore. All of that changed the day the "girl in the mirror" looked up at him and spoke. Chills ran down his spine as he realized that the reflection he had been seeing for the past ten years was a female version of him, and it seemed to be reaching out for help. This realization proved to be too much for the seventeen year old and he fainted.

Part Four:
Seeking What's Mine

Chapter 12

Elizabeth closed the door to her office and locked it. She stepped into the elevator and rode it to the parking garage where her car was waiting. It was a candy apple red, Mustang GT, convertible. She got in and pulled out of the garage, making her way to 2nd avenue, where there was a nice little Irish Pub that she frequented often. They served up the best lamb and potato stew, and they also made one hell of a Bloody Mary. She had her own table reserved in the back corner. The lighting had a dim romantic aura to it and with her field of vision she could see the entrance and the entire bar area. She glanced around and saw the usual crowd for a Friday night but as her eyes scanned across the bar, they came to rest on a handsome blonde haired blue eyed stranger. What Miss Evans wasn't aware of was this was no ordinary stranger. He knew her routine and he had been watching her for weeks from a distance. He knew what she would order, how many drinks she would have, how long she would stay and where she lived. He caught her eyeing him several times before they finally made eye contact. Their connection lasted long enough for him to smile at her. She nodded and smiled back. The stranger had the waitress take her a Bloody Mary and tell her it was from an admirer. He watched out of the corner of his eye until he was sure she was going to except it and then he got up and walked back to where she was sitting. When he reached the table, he had his hand outstretched and he introduced himself as Nate. When she reached up to shake his hand, he gently took her hand in his and kissed it ever so softly. He asked her for her name but really he already knew it. "My name is Elizabeth, nice to meet you Nate," was her reply. "Do you care if I join you for a few minutes," He asked? "No, not at all, she replied, but this is not a date." "Agreed, this is not a date, it is just a simple drink between new friends," He stated. "I wouldn't say friends either, I just met you and know nothing about you," She replied. "Well let's change that then. My full name is Nate McKinley. I am a newspaper journalist who is looking for a story," He told her. "What kind of story are you looking for Mr. McKinley?" "Please call me Nate, and I am not really sure but I will know it, when I find it," He said "Well Nate, it is nine o'clock and past time for me to be headed home, it was a pleasure to meet you. I guess I will see you around" She said, with a smile. "Maybe you will; maybe you won't. I have to follow the story you know" he replied back. "Right, I can't forget the story" she teased. "Well, take care of yourself, Nate" she said "You do the same, Elizabeth." He watched Miss Evans get into her car, and then he headed out of the pub himself.

Chapter 13

Nate drove around town for about an hour and then decided to go back to his hotel suite. He rode the elevator up to the third floor. He quietly walked down the narrow hallway, until he reached room 333. Once inside, he poured himself a shot of whiskey. He sat down on the sofa and took out his cellphone. He searched through his contacts and found the number he was looking for and hit the call button. The phone rang once and then it was answered. "This is Nate. I just wanted to let you know, that I made contact with Elizabeth tonight." "Great now we proceed as planned. I want that file. I don't care what it takes. Remember, Mr. McKinley, I am paying you for results and that is exactly what I want. You have a remarkable record as a Private Investigator, so don't let me down." "Don't worry sir; I will make sure you get what you paid for, goodnight." After pouring himself another shot, Nate got undressed and proceeded to take a steaming hot shower. Once he got out, he laid down on the bed, reached for the phonebook and searched for the number to the TDF&P. After programming the number into his speed dial, he set his alarm for eight a.m. Nate turned off his bedside lamp and laid there for what seemed like an eternity before he finally drifted off to dreamland. Once falling asleep, he slept like a baby. That is until his alarm woke him up.

Chapter 14

He got up and opened the blind expecting to see the sun shining into his room. Instead he saw the doom and gloom of an approaching thunderstorm on the horizon. That would not stop today's itinerary though, he thought to himself. He got dressed and sat on the edge of his bed and hit his speed dial number two. "Good morning Texas Department of Family and Protective services how may I direct your call?" "Is Miss Evans in the office today?" "Well normally she doesn't work on Saturday but today is your lucky day. May I ask who is calling?" "I am a potential client of hers. How late do you all stay open, today?" "The office closes at noon, but I am not sure of Miss Evans's agenda." "Well she isn't expecting me to call until Monday so I will just call her back then. She gave me a card with the direct line to her office but I seemed to have lost it, do you think you could give it to me again, please?" "Yes sir, it is 830-468-6662 ext. 3825, is there anything else I can do for you?" "No ma'am, that is all, thank you very much, have a great day." Nate looked into the mirror and said to himself, "Damn I'm good. I won't need this number for long though, by Monday evening, I will have her cell number." Nate stayed close to his hotel suite for most of the weekend, strategizing. He knew what he had to do but he couldn't lay all his cards down at one time because if he did, it would be game over. He was just about to doze off when his cell began to vibrate. He looked at the caller ID and decided to let it go to voicemail. His boss was intent on getting what he wanted but he really was a good guy. Even though the sun was barely setting, Nate decided that he would call it a day. He crawled into his bed, closed his eyes and let the sandman take him away. He tossed and turned most of the night because his mind was going ninety to nothing. He knew that if he pushed too hard he would lose his one chance of getting access to the file. Phase one of his plan was to get Elizabeth to fall for him. After that, he would just have to make it up as he goes.

Chapter 15

After rolling out of bed and getting ready for the day's events, Nate called the florist and had a huge bouquet of yellow and white daisies delivered to Miss Evans. The card simply said, "From your secret admirer." When Miss Evans read the card she immediately started smiling and the first person that came to his mind was Nate. "Hmmm, she thought to herself. "Wonder what kind of story he thinks he is going to find here? My daisies are beautiful though." She smelled them once more before setting them down. Then she began to wonder, "How did he know that daisies were my favorite kind of flower?" Before she could ponder on that thought for very long her phone began to ring. "Hello Elizabeth, I am so sorry to bother you at work but I was wondering if you got your flowers?" "Yes, I did, Mr. McKinley but you shouldn't have. I hope I didn't give you the wrong impression the other night but I don't have time for complications." "Please call me Nate and I am not trying to complicate anything. You were just so intriguing the other night and I wanted to thank you for allowing me the opportunity to sit with you. Did you like the daisies?" "Yes, they were beautiful. They are my favorite, how did you know?" "It was a lucky guess. I didn't peg you for the traditional rose kind of woman. Let me take you out to dinner tonight." "Nate you are a very nice guy but I just can't." "Oh right, I don't want to be a complication. Call me at 830-234-4231 if you change your mind." "Goodbye Nate." "Goodbye Miss Evans."

Chapter 16

After hanging up her phone, she cracked a smile. It was one of those, school girl crush, kind of smiles. No matter how hard she tried to get the blonde haired and blue eyed stranger out of her mind, she couldn't. No one had ever showed this kind of interest in her and she didn't know how to act or what to feel. A knock on her office door brought her back to reality. "Miss Evans I just wanted to let you know we heard from the Tennessee Department of Family and Protective Services and Katrina is doing exceptionally well." "Thank you, that really takes a load off of my mind." Then she thought to herself, "if only Jeffrey was." The rest of the day went by pretty fast for Elizabeth. She finished going through all of her files for the day and she logged out of her computer. Her eyes wondered towards her desk. She focused on the flowers she had received and the smile returned to her face. Against her better judgment, she pulled out her cell and dialed the number her admirer, Nate, had left her. He answered on the second ring. "This is Elizabeth, if it isn't too late, I would like to accept your offer for dinner, however, I do have a few conditions." "Anything, you name it." "I pick up my own check and you keep in mind this is just dinner." "You got it; just meet me at Texas Steak and More on the corner of Jefferson and Ridge Mont at Seven o'clock." "Great, I will see you there. Goodbye." "Nate had called and made reservations for two as soon as he talked to Elizabeth this morning. He figured if she declined he could just cancel them. It wasn't that he was being cocky; it was that he had high hopes. He was just a man that was used to getting what he wanted. He waited outside, until he saw the candy apple red, mustang pulling into the lot and then he went inside. When he saw her walk in, he had to rub his eyes and take a second look. Walking toward him was one of the most attractive women he had ever seen. She had on a red strapless sundress and matching high heels. The closer she got to their table the more beautiful she became. She had the perfect complexion. Her lips had a hint of light red lipstick, her eyes were a mesmerizing green and her reddish blonde hair flowed like a river down her back. The only way he could describe her was angelic. Once she made it to the table, they looked at the menu and they both ordered the house sirloin with baked potatoes and chef salad. Nate also ordered a bottle of their finest wine. He popped the cork and they sat and drank for hours, just talking and getting to know each other. However, they both agreed, this was not a date, it was just dinner. After finishing the whole bottle of wine Elizabeth was really feeling its effects, so she decided that it was time for her to go. She paid her check and Nate paid his. Nate walked her to her car, opened the door for her, leaned over and kissed her forehead then began walking away. He got about ten feet away when she called him back. Once he made it back to where she stood, they just stared at each other without saying a word. Then without warning he finally reached up and moved her hair off of her shoulder and ran his hand across her cheek. He leaned in and kissed her softly on her lips. The kiss only lasted for a few seconds but to her it would be remembered for a lifetime. That was what she wanted. That is why she called him back. She didn't want to admit it but this had been a date and it had been the best night of her life. He hugged her tight and before walking away for the second time he said, "The next non-date we have is on me." They both chuckled and they both disappeared into the night.

Chapter 17

Nate got to his suite and slid his key card into the slot. When he walked through the door he was immediately taken back by the scent and glow from a cigar. "For Christ's sake Mr. Ellis you startled me. How did you get in here," he asked? "I own the hotel and I make the keys." Bobby replied. "Well, what do you want?" "I came to see how things were progressing." "They are moving forward; just moving slower than I anticipated." "Well speed it up and don't go falling in love. I have been searching for my kids for nearly seventeen years and I will not rest until I find them." "Sir, with all due respect, you hired me to do a job and I will deliver, what you are paying me for." "Well glad we are on the same page." Mr. Ellis gets up and walks towards the door and then turns around and says, "Remember, you need to spend a little less time kissing and a little more time getting your hands on that file." Once Mr. Ellis left, Nate poured himself a stiff drink and called then it a night.

Chapter 18

The next morning, Elizabeth woke up in an exceptionally good mood. She got to work early, made coffee and sat at her desk admiring the daisies she received yesterday. Her mind drifted back to last night. She enjoyed the dinner, the wine and the talking, however, none of that put the smile on her face. Her mind was on the kiss. She had never been kissed with so much affection. She was in her own little world, when the phone rang and snapped her back into reality. She waited for the receptionist to answer it but it just kept ringing. Then it hit her, it was only seven thirty a. m. She answered it and said, "Hello." There was someone on the line, she could her them breathing but they wouldn't say anything. Her first thought was Nate but he had her cell number, so she just let it go. Her morning started out slow but it quickly turned into a busy one. All she wanted was another date but if it happened tonight it would be late. She checked her cell periodically throughout the morning and early afternoon, hoping to have had a missed call or a text from Nate but sadly she didn't have either as of yet. She was having difficulty concentrating; she just kept wondering, why he hadn't tried contacting her since last night.

Chapter 19

Nate had always been the type of person to finish what he started, but this time he was actually having second thoughts. He never dreamed that he would fall for one of his assignments. Nate wanted his cake but he also wanted to eat it. Meaning he wanted to finish his job but he also wanted the girl. He had to devise a plan so that he could achieve both. He thought about it for hours and then it hit him. "I will be a distraction and let someone else do the dirty work." He made a call to his boss and filled him in. Then he called her. She didn't answer but he left a message. "Elizabeth, its Nate, come by my suite tonight when you get off work. I really want to cook you dinner. Just text me if you can make it." He again just assumed she would so he took the opportunity to make his suite a little more romantic. He put a white tablecloth on the table and set it for dinner for two, complete with candles and wine glasses. He proceeded to the bathroom where he lined the garden style, Jacuzzi tub with candles. His last stop was his bed. He traded out his ordinary sheets for black satin and he threw rose petals everywhere. After his quick renovations he took a step back and admired his efforts. His phone vibrated and he looked at the display. It was a text that read: "I should wrap up around here by seven; I will see you at eight☺!" Nate closed his phone and grinned. Elizabeth was grinning as well. Now to send one final text, he said to himself. He typed: "She gets off at seven, her office is on the second floor, and she keeps the keys to her filing cabinet in her top left hand desk drawer. They are in alphabetical order. The one you want is labeled Jane and John Doe. Good luck. At about five minutes until eight, Nate took the pot roast casserole out of the oven and set it on the counter. He poured two glasses half full of vintage red wine. At eight o'clock sharp there was a knock on the door. Nate opened the door and gasped. He knew she was coming but she looked as if she were hand picked off the cover of the "sexiest bachelorette" edition of one of those weekly magazines. Her hair was in a tight French style braid, she was wearing an orange button up blouse, and blue jeans that fit snug enough to show every inch of her extraordinary and curvy figure. "Well aren't you going to invite me in?" "Oh I'm so sorry, where are my manners? Please come in." She sat her purse down on the counter and sat down at the table. Nate fixed their plates and he sat down with his date. They picked right up where they had left off last night. They drank, talked, giggled, ate, and drank some more. They finished eating and Elizabeth insisted on cleaning up from dinner. Nate sat at the table watching her wash the dishes. She looked sexy as hell, he thought to himself. He walked up behind her and put his hands around her waist. He leaned around her and kissed her on her neck. She sighed with approval. He gently spun her around where they were facing each other. He pulled her close and pressed his lips to hers. He began exploring the inside of her mouth with his tongue. He could feel her heart beating. He could tell she wanted him as much as he did her but he didn't want to rush things. He continued kissing her and finally took her by the hand and led her to his bedroom. Once in there, he sat her on the bed then reached up and pulled the pony tail holder out of her hair. She shook her head from side to side until the braid completely disappeared. He stood her up and moved her hair off her shoulders. He looked deep into her approving, green, eyes then he kissed her forehead. He moved to her cheek, then to her chin and then back to her lips. As he softly kissed her, he began unbuttoning her blouse from the bottom up. Once he got to the top button he slid his hands underneath the back of her blouse and unfastened her brassiere. He ran his hands over her breasts and as he did he felt her nipples harden in response. She reciprocated by lifting his T-shirt over his head, never breaking eye contact as it hit the floor. She reached down and felt his manhood and as it throbbed in her hand, she whispered "take me now" into his ear. They finished undressing each other and climbed into bed. She had never felt like this before, she had never had sex before. She believed in her heart this was right or at least it felt that way. Nate climbed atop of her slowly and gently inserted himself inside her. They once were two, but at the moment they were one. They made love for hours. After they had both climaxed for the last time, they just laid there cuddled in each other's arms, staring at one another. Nate got up and went into the bathroom, leaving Elizabeth lying in bed. Her whole body tingled from the inside out and her legs felt like spaghetti. She finally managed to stand without falling. She walked into the bathroom where Nate was sitting in the Jacuzzi that he lined in candles earlier. When he saw her he said, "So are you finally going to join me?" She smiled but before she could step over into the tub she heard her phone ringing. She walked back to the bedroom and answered it. "Hello Elizabeth, this is Detective Wallace I am calling to inform you that your office was broken into a few hours ago and whoever broke in really tore things up. Can you come down here?" "Yes give me just a few minutes." Elizabeth began getting dressed and as she was on her way back to the bathroom to tell Nate what was going on, she heard his phone vibrate on the bed side table. She normally wouldn't have looked at someone else's phone but her nerves were a mess. She opened his phone and read the text. It simply said, "We have the file." She lost all color in her face and when she looked up Nate was coming out of the bathroom in nothing but a towel. She threw his phone at him and told him about the break in. "I'm going to the office to talk to the police but before I do, I want to know what the hell is going on. Did you invite me over here so someone could break into my office? What file do they have? What am I in the middle of? Answer me dammit." "Calm down and let me explain." "Make it quick and it better be good or the police will have your name and instead of you finding a story, you will be the story."

Chapter 20

"Please Elizabeth sit down and hear me out. Let me finish before you say anything. My name really is Nate McKinley. I am not a reporter. I am…was a very good private investigator; however, I was fired because of a technicality. I went to school and got a degree in journalism but before I could get a job as a reporter, I got a phone call from this guy named Bobby Ellis. He told me he got my number from a friend and he wanted me to do a job for him. He told me that he had been looking for his kids for well over sixteen years and the only thing he had found out was the name of the case worker that handled their adoption. He paid me to follow you around and to learn your schedule. It wasn't by chance we met at the Irish Pub on 2nd Ave. What I didn't plan on was falling for you. I told him that I couldn't steal the file that he would have to get someone else to do it. The only thing I am guilty of is telling him that you would be here with me all night. That's the truth Elizabeth." She had tears running down her face. She looked up at him and said, "Do you realize what you have done? He signed over his parental rights nearly sixteen years ago. This was a closed adoption. If he contacts these families, I could lose my job. What does he hope to accomplish by finding them?" "He blames himself for the death of their birth mother and so does her father Mac. At first, Bobby just wanted to tell the kids who he was but Mac was recently diagnosed with early stages of cirrhosis of the liver and Bobby wanted to give the kids an opportunity to meet their maternal grandfather before it was too late." "If he would have approached me, I could have called and talked to their adoptive parents and given them the option of meeting him. Then everything would have been legal. Dammit! Nate, I will keep quiet where the police are concerned but it won't come without a price." "Anything, you name it." "You get me my file back, leave it on my door step and then leave town. I never want to see you again. Goodbye, Mr. McKinley, I will see myself out."

Chapter 21

"Hello officer, I am looking for Detective Wallace?" "He is standing right over there by the elevator ma'am." "Detective Wallace I am Elizabeth Evans." "Ah yes Miss Evans, well we are just about to wrap things up here. I have a couple quick questions for you. Do you know anyone who may have been targeting you for something? Your office was the only one broken in to and destroyed." "No not right off I can't." "Well can you tell just by looking if anything is missing?" "No, but it is a mess. Let me clean it up and then I will give you a call at the station." "Okay Miss Evans but as it stands we have no leads, no witnesses and no suspects, so if nothing is missing we will simply write it up as a suspicious vandalism. I will be waiting for your call." It took her nearly two hours to clean up and put everything back in its place. She was furious that Bobby hired someone to trash her office but at the same time she was relieved, because she knew who had done it, why and what it was that was taken. She kept her word and kept Nate and Bobby's name out of it. She called Detective Wallace and reported that nothing was missing. She hung the phone up and sat back in her chair. She reached across her desk, picked up her daisies and smelled them, and then she threw them against the wall. The vase shattered and the flowers scattered everywhere. She began sobbing and cursing the day she had ever met the blonde haired, blue eyed stranger.

Part Five:
Tying Up Loose Ends

Chapter 22

It had been a month since Elizabeth found the stolen file on her door step. Not only did she find the file but Nate had also left her a note. It said, **"*My dearest Elizabeth, I never meant to hurt you. My feelings for you were genuine, I just want you to know that I intercepted your file from the guy Bobby hired. He is pissed. I told him it was either the file or the police but he didn't take it any easier. I told him I came clean with you about everything and also told him what you said about doing things the legal way. I realize I messed up but please forgive me and except my sincerest apologies. You have my cell number. I will do as you have asked and I will stay away from you, just know that it pains me to do so; Yours Truly, Nate.*"** Elizabeth read his note every night, and every night she would cry herself to sleep. She had feelings for him but he betrayed her trust.

Chapter 23

Elizabeth woke up in a cold sweat. She felt sick to her stomach. She glanced at the clock and noticed it was only three a.m. She got up and went to the bathroom. She turned on the faucet to get her a drink of water, but before it ever hit her stomach, she was hugging the commode. She said to herself, "this can't be happening. I can't be coming down with a bug, not now." She puked so much that the only thing coming up was greenish brown bile and she was on verge of dry heaving. She wasn't a doctor but she knew if she didn't at least keep fluids down that she would become dehydrated. When she was finally able to stand up she walked to the kitchen and poured a small glass of ginger ale to sip on and got herself a few saltines. Finally, about four a.m., Elizabeth felt better and she made it back to bed. Her alarm went off at eight a.m. and she got out of bed, took shower, dressed and drove to work. She decided before the day got to hectic that she would call and check on J.J. She dialed the number and it began to ring. "Hello, Marianne speaking." "Hello Mrs. Jacks; It's Miss Evans, I was just calling to check on J.J." "It's the strangest thing, ever since he fainted, he has not seen the reflection and he doesn't have nightmares anymore. He spends more time with friends and he is doing exceptional." "That is great news Mrs. Jacks. I am extremely happy and relieved. Does Dr. Connor believe he has outgrown his phobias?" "Well he hasn't discharged him from his care just yet, but he has made the comment that it would appear the reflection or "girl in the mirror" if you will, is gone." "Thank you so much for your time and the wonderful news Mrs. Jacks. Take care and goodbye." "Goodbye Miss Evans." Just about the time she hung up the phone, her receptionist brought in her usual French Vanilla Cappuccino. She got the words thank you out of her mouth but the sweet vanilla smell made her stomach turn. She jumped up and ran to her bathroom, barely making it to the toilet and up came her ginger ale and saltines. She told Jill, her receptionist, that she thought she had a stomach bug and to cancel all her appointments. She also had her call Dr. Olivia Jones, to see about setting her up an appointment.

Chapter 24

"Miss Evans, Dr. Jones said she would work you in. She said to tell you just to come on in." "Thanks Jill. Please cancel all my appointments for the rest of the week." "Yes Ma'am, hope you get to feeling better." Elizabeth pulled her mustang into an empty parking place, right in front of the Women's Clinic. She walked up to the little window and signed in, showed her insurance card and headed to the waiting area. Before she even sat down, she heard Olivia say, "Come on back Elizabeth. What is going on with you?" "I really think that I have some kind of bug. I have vomited so much, I have nothing left in me." "Have you had any fever? Cough?" "No, neither one." "Let us take a blood sample and we will go from there." Elizabeth sat and waited for her doctor and good friend to return. Nearly fifteen minutes past before Olivia came back in. "Well, is it something antibiotics can fix, she asked?" "Not exactly, Elizabeth." "Okay your scaring me, just tell me, what is it? "Your...your pregnant! I believe you are experiencing morning sickness." Elizabeth didn't know what to say. Tears welled up in her eyes and began flowing down her cheeks. She slowly got up and walked out of the clinic but before she made it to the car she was dry heaving again. This time it was anxiety. She had to call the one person that she didn't ever want to see again. She had to call Nate. She left the parking lot and stopped by the local dollar store and purchased a home pregnancy test. It wasn't that she didn't believe her friend and doctor but she wanted to see for herself. She put the pedal to the metal and had the 5.0 whipping in the wind. She ran into the house and went straight to the bathroom. She pissed on the end of the stick and didn't have to wait long before a dark pink plus sign appeared in the little window. She now knew it was real. She had a life growing inside of her and her life would never be the same. She called Nate's cell and left him a message that said, *"Something has happened and I need to see you immediately. Don't bother calling me just get your ass over here as soon as you get this message. I don't care what time because I am off all week."*

Chapter 25

It had been two hours since she had left the message on Nate's cell, and still no word. Elizabeth undressed and slipped into her "jammies." That is what she called her sleep shorts and t-shirt. She wore her jammies often because they were comfortable and allowed her breasts the opportunity to breathe. She grabbed the remote control and flipped thru the channels but nothing was on or at least anything that would take her mind off of him. Yes, she was upset at him but she couldn't get him out of her mind. The time they spent together was nothing short of magical. However, she also couldn't help but think it was all just a plan to get information. Tonight she would get her answer. She had just gotten up and went to the bathroom when she heard a knock at the door. She looked out the peep hole and her heart skipped a beat. It was him. She opened the door and invited him in. He came in and sat down. He spoke first. "I didn't expect to hear from you after our last face to face." "Well I have had time to think and I wanted to ask you something." "Ask me anything, I swear I will be honest." "Were you serious when you said you fell for me and wanted to be with me? Are your feelings for me genuine?" "Oh, Elizabeth you have no idea. I fell hard for you. I love you." "Well you have eight months to prove it." "Eight months, what are you saying?" "Here this should make it a little clearer." She hands him the home pregnancy test and watches for his reaction. At first, he just sits there dumbfounded or stunned. Then, it hits him, "this is the reason she called me." Tears began to form in his eyes. He got up and pulled her to her feet. He wrapped his arms around her waist and whispered "just wait and see. I will be the best father ever." "You bet your ass you will." She allowed him to kiss her lips, just as he did the very first time. It was soft and slow and very passionate. She asked him to stay the night with her and his answer was "Miss Evans, yes I will stay the night with you tonight and every night for the rest of our lives." "Mr. McKinley, Is that your way of asking me to marry you?" "If it was, would you say yes?" "Well, Mrs. McKinley does have a nice ring to it," she teased.

Chapter 26

The next morning Bobby called Elizabeth's cell. She didn't recognize the number but she answered it anyway. "Hello." "Miss Evans, please, do not hang up. I have been doing a lot of thinking over the past few weeks. I know I went about everything all wrong. I was desperate. I just wanted to try and make things right. I do feel responsible for Melanie's death and I thought if I could find the kids and bring them to Mac he would forgive me." "Bobby, I understand what you're saying but you are undermining Melanie's wishes. She made this a closed adoption for a reason. They will be eighteen in less than a year from now and then their file will become public record. I realize you have spent years looking for them and I am sorry for that but under the circumstances, I think you can wait a little while longer." "Please, If not for me, do it for Mac." "I will call their parents and leave it up to them. That is the best I can do. I am not promising anything." "Thank you Miss Evans, Goodbye." Bobby was not done plotting. He had an inside contact at the phone company. He instructed her to get him the phone bill summary for Elizabeth Evans. He went over the summary with a fine tooth comb. There were two numbers that stood out. So he done a reverse search and got the names and addresses for a Mr. and Mrs. Jacks and a Mr. and Mrs. Hall. "Sorry Mel, but I need my kids to know the truth. I was forced to sign over my rights," He said to himself.

Part Six:
Seek and Ye Shall Find

Chapter 27

Bobby continued researching the addresses; he had gotten from the cellphone bill summary. To his surprise, one of the addresses was only a half hour away. Instead of going there first, he decided he would take a trip to Tennessee and pay a visit to Mr. and Mrs. Hall. After doing a few calculations he figured the trip to be 666 miles by plane or 784 miles by car. Bobby was extremely superstitious so he chose to drive. It would take him fourteen hours to arrive at the address. He thought that would give him plenty of time to come up with a plan. He didn't know which one of his kids he was going to discover first or how they would receive him but now that he had located them he had to try. Once he arrived in Nashville, he began looking for a place to set up house. He pulled into the parking lot of the Opry Mills Hotel and that is where he decided he would sleep or at least for the night. What Bobby didn't know was he wasn't alone; he had been followed to Tennessee. Someone was going to make sure that he didn't do anything that he would come to regret in the long run. The next morning, Bobby was sitting in the lobby of the hotel. He was reading the Nashville Gazette while drinking a cup of black coffee he got from the free continental breakfast bar. He felt as if he were being watched but there were no other guests in the lobby area but him. He finished the coffee and folded the paper in half and pitched it back down onto the table. He walked to his car typed in the address belonging to

Mr. and Mrs. Hall then pulled out of the lot. It took twenty minutes to arrive at the address that was typed into the GPS. He simply drove on by after confirming that he had found the house. He thought to himself," I will come back after the sun sets and maybe I will get a glimpse of one of my children". He returned to his room and decided he would shower and shave.

Chapter 28

"Hello Mac! You were right. Bobby is up to no good. He drove by a house earlier and I have a feeling that he is going back tonight." "Listen, old friend; don't let him interfere with Mel's last wishes. Oh and please don't let him know we are on to him." "You got it Mac. He won't know what hit him". Later on that evening, just as expected, Bobby drove back to the address. He watched the house from afar off at first but then he began inching closer and closer. Just as he was approaching the living room window to take a peek inside, a Louisville Slugger caught him right across the back of his skull. Bobby fell forward lifeless. It wasn't long until the ambulance and the police descended upon the address. When they simultaneously pulled up Mr. and Mrs. Hall and their daughter Katrina walked outside shocked to find a man lying face down under their living room window, bleeding heavily. The officer on the scene reached into the back pocket of the bleeding man and retrieved his identification then allowed the paramedics to do their job. The officer examined the victim's driver's license and found it belonged to a Bobby Ellis of Houston Texas. He ran the license number and it came back clean. He was a hotel owner there. The officer asked himself several questions including, "Why is he here in Nashville? What was he doing at this residence? And what the hell happened here? The answer to these questions would have to wait. The victim seemed to have suffered a major blow to the head causing swelling of the brain, a severe concussion, and as of now, he is listed in critical condition. Jerry called his friend. "Mac, Bobby is in bad shape. Apparently he was trespassing and took a major blow to the head from a ball bat. They say he is in critical condition. I think now it would be a good idea to contact Miss Evans and let her know what he has been up to." "Thanks Jerry. Now get your ass back to Texas and destroy any evidence you have. I'm your alibi if you need one. We were fishing." Mac hung up the phone and realized his pal was right. He had to call Miss Evans and let her know what was going on. He found the number to her office and decided he would call her first thing in the morning.

Chapter 29

When Mac woke the next morning he took a shower and got dressed. He made his way to the kitchen where he smelled a heavenly scent. It was a pot of freshly brewed coffee made from authentic Columbian coffee beans. He also found a note on the table that Mary had left for him. *"**Dear Mac, I had to run a few errands I will be back soon. I fixed a pot a coffee and there are Cheese Danishes in the oven. I even took the liberty of fetching you the morning paper. Please follow the doctor's orders and don't overdo it. I love you, Sis.**"* After his third cup of coffee and second Danish he decided to call Miss Evans.

Chapter 30

"Come in Miss Evans thank you for agreeing to see me on such short notice." "Well Mr. Coleman you didn't leave me much choice." "Please call me Mac. I am sorry if I sounded demanding but I need to share some information with you. Information I think you will want to hear. Can I offer you a cup of coffee or Danish?" "No thank you, Mac. If you don't mind, just get to the reason you called me here." "Fair enough. May I call you Elizabeth?" "Yes, please do." "Well as you are aware, I am Melanie's dad. I have always blamed Bobby for her death. He left the hospital while I was in a coma and wasn't seen or heard from for years. Recently he came to me and tried apologizing and I threw him out but not before he told me he had been looking for his kids. He told me that he didn't have much of a lead but that he learned the name of their case worker. I knew then he would not stop until he found them, completely undermining Melanie's wishes. So I called a friend of mine, Jerry, and had him start following Bobby around. We illegally planted a bug in his car and heard him talking to a private investigator about stealing a file. Several days later Bobby became furious when the P.I. told him to get someone else. He did just that. Bobby called Slim. He was a known drug user and Bobby bribed him with a small score. Jerry watched him break into your office and come out with a file. However, before he could get the file to Bobby, someone intercepted it. That ticked Bobby off and he then tried calling you to apologize and to get you to call the kids' parents. When you told him about the records eventually becoming public he assumed you wouldn't help. So he called in a favor to a gal-pal of his, who worked for the phone company...She gave him a bill summary of all your calls over the last five years. By simple deduction he eliminated all the numbers until he found what he had been hoping for. Two days ago, Jerry followed him to Nashville and saw him lurking outside the house of Mr. and Mrs. Hall. He handled the situation and made sure Bobby didn't make contact with the family." "Where is Bobby now?" "Well...he is in a Trauma Center in critical condition." "Why tell me all this and what makes you think I won't go to the authorities?" "Elizabeth I know you won't go to the cops with this. For one, you obstructed justice by covering up the break in at your office and second, you don't want Bobby finding his kids any more than I do." "You are right Mac. I have watched these kids grow and mature and I can't allow my job to be jeopardized by a self-centered bastard. So what do we do now Mac?" "You don't do anything Elizabeth. Leave Bobby to me and you take care of yourself." "Mac, can I ask you a question?" "Yes anything?" "Do you have cirrhosis of the liver?" "No, I do have a rare liver infection that I am having trouble fighting off but I'm not in any danger of dying anytime soon, despite what Bobby has claimed." "Do you ever wonder about your grandkids?" "Honestly I think about them daily but I have to respect my daughter's wishes. I was mad and hurt when she first got pregnant but I was kind of hoping she would have changed her mind at the last minute about giving them up but, well you know what happened." Elizabeth took Mac's hand and looked him in the eye. "Mac I want you to know that Katrina and Jeffrey are safe and they are being well taken care of. They look a lot like Melanie. I hope for your sake that your grandkids get a chance to meet you. Can I please use your bathroom?" "Of course, Elizabeth, it is down the hall second door on the left." Once Elizabeth closed the door to the bathroom, she let the tears flow. She couldn't believe the lengths Bobby went to in order to undermine Melanie's wishes and at the same time she couldn't believe the lengths Mac went to, to protect them. She washed her face and then returned to the kitchen where she found Mac sitting at the table looking at an 8x10 picture of his daughter taken just before she died. His eyes were red and swollen and Elizabeth knew he had been crying. She patted him on the back before walking to the door. "Mac, I have never lost anyone but I have always heard that as long as you keep their memory alive and you focus on the good times the pain eventually eases up. Goodbye Mac." "Goodbye Elizabeth." Mac looked at the picture of his daughter one more time. He ran his fingers across her abdomen and smiled as he uttered two words, "Katrina and Jeffrey."

Part Seven:
Sometimes Dreams Do Come True

Chapter 31

The sky was clear and blue; there was not a cloud in site. The wind was relatively calm except for a slight warm breeze blowing. Katrina thought to herself that it would be a perfect day to sit in the bleachers and to catch up on her English Composition assignment. She chose to do a paper on the physical expectations and physical limitations of athletes, based on weight, height, sex and type of sport. So she thought what better way to start than to watch from the sidelines as the football team was preparing for their scrimmage game. What she did not realize was that she was fixing to have a front row seat to one of the biggest break-ups of her senior year. She watched as Tiffany walked right onto the field and right up to Tommy. She slapped him and called him a cheating bastard. He never said a word as she turned and walked away. It wasn't until she yelled at Katrina, asking if she enjoyed the show that he turned and lifted his eyes up in her direction. He smiled at her, put his helmet on and said, "Let's do this fella's shall we!" She decided that maybe it wasn't a good day to do her assignment after all so she headed home.

Chapter 32

Once she got home she done her chores and then went to her room. She was getting her homework assignments together but something stopped her. She couldn't stop thinking about Tommy smiling at her. She had developed a crush on him from the moment she saw him her freshmen year but she knew that he was out of her league. She was a "nerd" so to speak. She was at the top of her class and took her school work very seriously. She wasn't into sports of any kind and he was the starting quarterback. Tiffany, the captain of the cheer squad, swooped in and laid claim on him so Katrina let her crush on him be just that, a crush. She never told anyone except for her diary. She reached between the mattresses of her bed and retrieved it, and then she proceeded to add this entry. **_"Dear diary sometimes dreams do come true. Tommy smiled at me today. It was just a brief smile but a smile none the less. Oh and Tiffany broke up with him. I am all smiles."_** She closed her diary and replaced it back where it was. Her mother knocked on her door to let her know dinner was on the table. After supper she cleaned up and then returned to her room and her homework. After finishing her homework she crawled into bed, closed her eyes and again thought back to this afternoon when Tommy smiled at her and she drifted off to sleep.

Chapter 33

A knock on her bedroom door woke Katrina. "I'm up mom." "Okay honey, there is cereal, toast and juice on the table." "Thanks, I am going to jump in the shower then I will be right out." Kat stretched and made her way to her bathroom. She decided to fore go the norm this morning. Instead of jeans and a t-shirt she opted for a pair of black slacks and a hunter green V-neck blouse. Instead of her hair being pulled up into a pony tail she opted to straighten it and let it flow down her back. Once she was dressed and her hair was done she looked into the mirror, shrugged, and said, "What the hell?" She was going to go all out this morning. She decided that after three and a half years of not wearing make-up in high school this would be the morning. She painted her face and traded in her spectacles for contacts. When she finally finished getting ready she looked into the full length mirror hanging on her closet door and grinned from ear to ear. She knew she would turn heads but there was only one head she wanted to turn. She grabbed her diary and wrote a quick entry. ***"Today this ugly duckling has been transformed into a swan."*** She returned the diary to its normal place, ran through the kitchen, grabbing a piece of toast and a bottle of orange juice on her way out the door.

Chapter 34

Katrina was right in her assumption that she would turn heads. As she walked down the hall on the way to her locker, every person she came into contact with had to take a second look. They looked at her as if she were a new student entering the school for the very first time. When she finally made it to her locker, Tommy was standing at the end of the hall eying her. She tried hard not to make eye contact with him. She kept looking down at the floor. She noticed a pair of shoes walking toward her and when she looked up, Tommy was standing not more than two foot away. "Hey, Kat you look absolutely stunning. Would you like to go to the Fall Formal with me Friday night?" She was thinking to herself, she would love too but she did not want to sound desperate. "I don't know if that would be a good idea Tommy." "Why would it not be a good idea?" "Well for starters, Tiffany just broke up with you yesterday and I don't want to be a re-bound girl and second I have been told when it comes to dancing that I have two left feet." "Then that's perfect because I have two rights." "I am not saying yes but I will consider it." "Good, I will be waiting for your answer." He smiled at her as he walked away, and for a brief moment she closed her eyes and imagined herself being swept off her feet on the dance floor. That image was short lived. Tiffany walked up to her and said, "Just because you dressed up and put on a little make-up doesn't change the fact that you're still a geek. I may not be with Tommy right now but bitch you better keep your distance or else." Katrina got toe to toe with Tiffany and replied, "Or else, what?" Tiffany didn't have time to answer before the principal came out of his office and said, "Ladies, I suggest you put your differences aside and get to class." Tiffany mumbled under her breath as she walked away, "This isn't over Sleeping Beauty, you better find yourself another prince." Katrina thought about what Tiffany had mumbled, all day. The more she thought about it the more pissed off she became. She knew exactly what she was going to do. The last bell rang and she was the first one out the door. She ran down the hall to Tommy's locker and waited for him. It was Wednesday and she knew he didn't have practice. The coach believed in giving God his due. She finally got a glimpse of him and his "boy's" heading her way. By "boy's" she was referring to Steven and Scottie. Normally, where you saw one, you saw all three. That was their motto, "One for all and all for one." Once they reached Tommy's locker the other two boys stepped aside and let Tommy have his space. "So Kat, to what do I owe this honor?" "Well I've thought about it all day and I have decided that I would love to go to the Fall Formal with you." That put a smile on his face. He replied with, "Awesome I can't wait." "Can't wait for what," came from out of nowhere. They all turned to see Tiffany standing there. Well, not that it is any of your business but Katrina has agreed to be my date for the dance Friday night. Tiffany glanced at her with a look of pure hatred. Katrina turned, walked to her locker, grabbed her purse, and left the school with the biggest smile on her face and the greatest sense of satisfaction. She thought to herself, "Mission accomplished."

Chapter 35

She was still glowing when she walked into her house. Her mom noticed the grin on her face and was delighted that her daughter was actually smiling for a change. Katrina went to her room and pulled out her diary and entered two entries. Entry number one said, ***"Tommy asked me to the dance today." Entry number two said, "I stood my ground today and successfully made an enemy."*** She put her diary up and went to the kitchen to help her mother with supper. "Hey honey. How was your day? I couldn't help but notice you were smiling when you came in and you look so beautiful." "Mom, I was asked to go to the Fall Formal today and I accepted." "That's wonderful Kat. You deserve to have a little fun. You study nonstop and I was starting to think you didn't have a social life." "Well I didn't before today, but you're right, I do need to let loose just a little bit." They finished cooking supper and setting the table just in time for her dad to walk through the door. "Hey sweetheart, who is that pretty young lady, helping you with dinner?" "You're so funny dad. It is me Kat." "Well you look different with your hair down, contacts in and make-up on. Do I have a reason to be worried?" "No dad, I am just growing up and it is time I acted like it." They sat down at the table, her dad said grace, and they ate together, just as a family should. They all three realized that they lived in the fast lane and that they only had a few minutes to actually see each other before starting their days, but they made sure that every night that they sat around the dinner table and interacted with each other. After dinner Katrina excused herself and went to her room. She had two days to find a dress and to get her English paper done. She flipped through a clothing catalog but couldn't really find what she was looking for, so she decided she would go to Tuxedos and More, after school tomorrow. She finished what she could on her paper, set her alarm and drifted off to sleep.

Chapter 36

Katrina woke up early and got ready for school. She grabbed herself a pop tart and headed out the door. She figured that she would get to school and stop by the library before her first class started. She still had her report to finish that would count as fifty percent of her English Comp grade. After checking out what she needed, she swung by her locker. When she opened her locker she found a note. It simply said, **_"Sleeping Beauty, I told you to find yourself another Prince Charming, guess now you will have to face my wrath."_** Katrina grinned after reading it and then she threw it away. She wasn't scared but she did look over her shoulder for the rest of the day, however, Tiffany remained M.I.A. She really didn't care one way or the other. Despite being verbally abused by a selfish, no good hussy, Katrina was determined to keep the smile on her face. She giggled as she thought back to the moment Tommy let the news of her being his date just flow loosely from his lips.

Chapter 37

Katrina pulled out of the school parking lot and headed south towards Tuxedos and More. She arrived at her destination, pulled into a vacant parking space and headed for the entrance. Before she even entered the store, she spotted the perfect dress. It was hanging on a life-like mannequin in the left, store front, display window. The dress was teal in color, it was strapless and the length wasn't too long nor was it too short. It wasn't plain Jane but it wasn't too formal either. The only way to describe it was perfect. The only thing left for her to do was find a store employee that could assist her. She began looking around and ran into someone. "Hi my name is Missy, how may I help you?" "Well I was interested in the teal dress in the window." "That is the last one we have in stock, in that color." "Please tell me it is a women's size four." "Well, as a matter of fact I do believe it is." "That's awesome I will take it." Katrina swiped her card for the dress and matching shoes then exited the store. She hung her dress up on the clothing hook behind the driver's seat and pitched her shoes into the floorboard. She started the engine up and it occurred to her, "Sometimes dreams do come true." She put her car into reverse and headed home.

Part Eight: Cruel Intentions

Chapter 38

"Hey Craig this is T call me back. I know you are screening your calls but I need that favor now." Fifteen minutes later T's phone rang. "What kind of favor do you need?" "Can you still get access to Ketamine?" "Yeah I think so. When do you need it?" "I need it tonight and I also got a job for you. You are going to take provocative pictures of one of my hot classmates." "Wait just a freaking minute. You are going to drug someone and you want me to take photos of them." "Yes that's right. Then you will drive her one block away from her house and leave her in her car." "Are you insane?" "Maybe, I am, but you will do this or I will spill the beans about your little gay rendezvous with a certain lacrosse player." "You wouldn't dare!" "Then meet me at my house tonight with the ketamine." "Do I need to dress up?" "You idiot, just be here by six o'clock pm. Once Tiffany finished getting ready she looked at her watch. "Dammit, where is Craig? It is five minutes 'til six and no sign of him," she said aloud. She had all but given up on him, when she spotted his blue Chevy S10 pickup making its way down her street. He pulled into her drive way, jumped out and said, "Am I good or what? It is six o'clock sharp. Damn T, you are looking hot tonight. Hot with a capital H. Orange is definitely your color." "Shut up loser. Come inside and let's go over the plan." They make their way into the living room where T begins to divulge the plan. "Okay, listen up. Here is how this is going to go down. You are going to leave your truck parked in the lot behind the Roberto's Mexican restaurant. You will ride with me to the dance. Since the cheer squad is sponsoring the Fall Formal, I have arranged to have valet parking. That is how you will gain access to Katrina's keys. I will pretend to bury the hatchet with her and insist she try the punch. The effects of the Ketamine are almost instantaneous. Once she starts feeling a little faint so to speak, I will send you to get her car. You will drive her to the Holiday Inn on 2nd and Commerce, where I have a room reserved under Mr. & Mrs. Smith. Strip her down butt naked and take several photos with my digital camera and be sure to include her face. Then redress her and take her and her car to the lot where your truck is at. Make your way back here and give me my camera. You will then finish your night as "Mr. Valet." Do you have any questions?" "What happens if someone sees me?" "Then I play dumb. I will say I don't know why a loser, dropout, showed up at our dance." "Has anyone ever told you that you are such a bitch." "Ha, yes, as a matter of fact I get that quite often. Are you ready to get this show on the road?" "I guess but just know if I go down, so do you, you best believe that." She throws a Tux at him and says, "Get dressed and let's go. Oh and one more thing, don't ever threaten me again or you will see just how big a bitch I can be." "Just so we are clear I didn't threaten you sweetheart, I just made you a promise." See the thing is Craig just caught their whole conversation on a pocket recorder. He learned a long time ago that if you dance with the devil, you are going to get burned but this time around things were going to be different, this time around he was going to be the devil.

Chapter 39

They dropped off Craig's truck and headed to the dance. As expected the dance was just beginning to get started and Tommy hadn't arrived yet. He never was one for punctuality. She spotted Katrina pulling into the school's circular drive. She nudged Craig and sent him to get her keys. "This is it, she thought. She went to the punch bowl and got two cups. She dropped a dose of Ketamine into one of the cups and waited for Katrina to make her grand entrance. Once she was inside, Tiffany didn't waste a single minute. She ran right up to her and began apologizing for everything. She played the victim and said she was just hurt and she was sorry for taking things out on her. Katrina was very forgiving but also very gullible. She bought Tiffany's story: hook, line and sinker. They hugged and Tiffany offered her a cup of punch. Katrina took the cup and so kindly said, "you didn't poison it did you?" Tiffany just grinned and they both turned their cups bottom side up. The new pals stood around making small talk for about ten minutes. That's when Tiffany noticed that Katrina began shaking like she had caught a chill. She acted concerned and asked if she was alright. Katrina told her she felt nauseated and felt like she might pass out. She called Craig and had him pull Katrina's car around. Tiffany was the only person authorized to wonder in and out of the school because she was overseeing the Valet Parking booth. The faculty chaperoning this dance trusted their students perhaps a little too much. She walked Katrina to her car and opened the passenger door. She introduced Craig as John Smith, her cousin, and assured her that he would get her home safe. Katrina was really incoherent. Tiffany handed Craig her keycard for room 111 at the Holiday Inn. "Get her home and then get back here," she said as she winked at him.

Chapter 40

By the time they left the school, Katrina was in and out of consciousness and completely unaware of what was happening. They made it to the hotel and Craig tried to rouse her but to no avail. He made sure the coast was clear, then picked her up and carried her into the room, the way a groom would carry his new bride. He laid her motionless body onto the bed and closed the door. He took off her dress revealing her bra and panties. He watched her lying there for several minutes and realized he needed to get this over with. He slowly unfastened her bra and then slid her panties down her long slender legs. He took out the camera and began taking snapshot after snapshot. She began to convulse just a little so he decided to hurry the process up just a bit. He took several more shots of her uncovered flesh making sure to include her beautiful face. She must have started getting cotton mouth because she began licking her lips. He got one shot with her eyes half opened and an expression on her face, as if she had just climaxed. He decided he would let that be the money shot. He put the camera down and just starred, watching her in all her glory. He glanced at his wrist and realized he had spent a little too much time completing the task at hand. He raised her up to a sitting position and her arms fell around his neck, as if she were hugging him. The scent of her perfume hit him and he knew he had to get out of that hotel quick before he done something he would surely regret. He managed to get her bra and panties back on fairly easy and after a brief struggle with her dress she again was fully clothed. After double checking to make sure the coast was still clear, he carried her back to the car. He then drove to the lot behind Roberto's. He got out and gently laid her down in the back seat of her car and walked away. Once in his truck, Craig breathed a huge sigh of relief. Not only was this night almost officially over but he and Tiffany were now even. No one would ever find out about his encounter with a certain lacrosse player. He looked around and saw that he was all alone on the roadway so he kicked it into high gear, wasting no time getting the camera back.

Chapter 41

Tiffany checked the time on her phone. It had been about an hour, since Craig left with Katrina, he should be back anytime. She was just about to turn and go back inside when she saw Tommy pull in. He never let anyone drive his '79 Cutlass Supreme, not even his boy's. So she waited for him to park his own car and walk toward the entrance. "Hey Tommy, I'm sorry to tell you but your date left sick." Tommy looked at her with a questioning expression on his face but realized something must've been wrong because Katrina wouldn't answer his repeated phone calls. He decided to stay and mingle but he made it clear to Tiffany that she was no longer a part of his life and never would be again. This truly hurt her but at the same time enraged her even more. However, she knew that soon enough she would have the last laugh. Soon, very soon, Katrina will be exposed for all to see. Craig pulled back up at the school and started helping the other valet attendant pull cars around lining them up in the order they were parked. He had just gotten out of his last vehicle when Tiffany came back out. She motioned for him. He came to where she was at, away from everyone who was exiting. He handed her the camera and reminded her that they were even. He also made sure to reiterate that if things went south then he wasn't going down alone. She told him they were through and she hoped she never had to see his face again. He began walking back to his truck then suddenly stopped. He turned around and said, "Hey, you're welcome." She rolled her eyes then took the camera and put it in her purse. After everything was cleaned up at school and everyone had left, Tiffany decided she would head home as well.

Chapter 42

She jumped into the shower, and as she stood under the stream of water letting the warmth run down her body, she couldn't help but recall the last few hours. She couldn't wait to see the photos that were on her camera. She got out of the shower, dried off, grabbed her purse and started scrolling through her pictures. She thought to herself, "Craig has really exceeded my expectations." She was in awe as she continued scrolling. She again thought aloud, "Katrina is just as beautiful in the buff as she is fully dressed. Everyone is going to get to experience her beauty."

Chapter 43

A patrol officer was patrolling the streets and noticed a car sitting in an empty parking lot in a handicap space. It didn't have a handicap sticker or a placard hanging from the rearview so he pulled around behind it and turned on his flashing lights. He ran the tag number and it came back to a Katrina Hall. He was about to ask for a number or address when he seen movement in the back seat. He put his hand on his gun and moved in closer. He got to the back passenger door and shined his light inside. He saw a girl lying in the back seat wearing a Teal dress. He asked her for her name but she couldn't answer him. She just kept mumbling. He asked her if she had been drinking and again she couldn't respond. He called it in and asked for an ambulance to be dispatched to the parking lot behind the Roberto's Mexican restaurant. He also requested an officer to go by her house and alert her parents. The ambulance arrived and after a quick exam they determined it would be best to take her to the hospital as a safety precaution. She was borderline dehydrated but they knew something else was going on. She was too disoriented to just be dehydrated. The ambulance arrived at the hospital in about ten minutes. Katrina's stats were all fine except for an increased heart rate. She was still not very alert. She kept mumbling and the only thing anyone could make out was, Tommy. The paramedics had already hooked her up to an IV, so the ER doctors ordered urinalysis and a toxicology report.

Chapter 44

While they were waiting for the results, Mr. and Mrs. Hall showed up demanding to see their daughter. One of the nurses ushered them into an eight by eight room and there they saw their 17 year old baby girl lying there motionless and slightly pale. A doctor poked his head around the curtain that divided one bed from the other, when he heard them talking to her. He told them that her test results should be back momentarily. He also assured them not to worry because she was going to be fine. The doctor came in after about a fifteen minute delay and told Mr. and Mrs. Hall that he had the results of their daughters' tests. He explained to them that she had ingested a very powerful drug known as Ketamine. When questioned about the drug, the doctor explained to them that it was primarily used as an anesthetic in most veterinarian clinics. He went on to explain that some individuals use this drug as a date rape drug due to the fact that it is very fast acting and it affects a person's ability to remember anything or anyone for a short length of time. "Was my daughter raped?" "There was no evidence of rape but paramedics did notice that her panties had been removed and then replaced." "What makes them think that?" "Well, they stated that they were put on her backwards." "Dear Jesus, when can we take our daughter home?" "Let us make sure she gets all her IV fluids. We would also like her to become alert enough to tell us her name and what year it is." "The police want to speak with you both for a few minutes." "Yes, of course." "Mr. and Mrs. Hall, I am Detective Collins and this is Detective Givens. We want to ask you a few questions. Do you know anyone who would want to harm your daughter?" "No, she charms everyone she comes into contact with." "The paramedics said she kept mumbling Tommy. Who is Tommy?" "It is a guy she met from school. I think he is the starting quarterback for the football team. He was also supposed to be her date for the Fall Formal." "Thank you, we will keep in touch. Oh, if Katrina remembers anything, anything at all, no matter how insignificant she thinks it is, please call us." The Detectives headed for the elevator with a new piece of the puzzle.

Chapter 45

Meanwhile, The Hall's went back to check on their daughter. When they made it to her room, she was sitting up with support from the hospital bed. She was still weak and groggy. She complained of a severe headache, border lining on a migraine. On the outside she looked like an angel but the drug was taking its toll on her from the inside. It was now midnight and she had no recollection of what had occurred over the last few hours. She asked, "What happened?" Her parents began filling her in. The last thing Katrina remembered about the last night was giving her keys to a valet attendant in front of the school. She continued drifting in and out of sleep. Finally about two thirty in the morning she was discharged from the hospital.

Chapter 46

Detectives Collins and Givens decided to wait until daybreak before talking to Tommy. They showed up at his residence and began knocking on the door. Tommy wasn't modest in the least; he answered the door in his boxer briefs. Det. Collins introduced himself and his partner, and then asked Tommy to get dressed, so that they could ask him a few questions. He agreed and went and slipped into a pair of jeans. When he returned he had a shit eating grin on his face and said sarcastically, "So officers what did I do?" Its Detectives and we are not accusing you of anything. We are going to ask you a few questions if that's okay? Do you know Katrina Hall?" His expression immediately changed from sarcasm to real concern. "Yes, she is a very attractive girl from my school. She was supposed to be my date at the Fall Formal last night but I was running late. When I got there Tiffany told me she left sick. She said she was only there for like twenty minutes. I tried calling her four or five times but couldn't get thru." "Can anyone corroborate your story?" "Yes I was with my boys, Steven and Scottie." "Hmmm, said Det. Givens, isn't Scottie's father a veterinarian?" "Yes, but why is that relevant?" "Well Katrina was drugged last night. Someone slipped a dose of Ketamine into her drink, at some point. Ketamine is used as an anesthetic in animal clinics and veterinarian offices. It is also used by date rapists because the effects are five time faster than GHB and others that are on the market." The detectives again noticed the concerned look on Tommy's face. "Look, I like Katrina and I would never drug her, especially with the intent of raping her." "We believe you son. We also don't believe rape was the motive for the drugging. We have one more question. Has Scottie ever mentioned his father having an internship program?" "Yes but the program excluded immediate family members. However, he had two other boys in the program. Tyler and Craig were their names best I can remember. They were big time lacrosse players." "You said, had." "Well rumor has it that Craig started experimenting with different recreational drugs. His grades began to slip and he was eventually kicked off the lacrosse team. One of the rules of the internship was maintaining your grade point average. When Scottie's dad got wind of Craig's grades he kicked him out of the program. After being kicked of the team and out of the program Craig dropped out of school all together. Tyler, on the other hand, finished the program and still works for him from time to time when he is home from college." "Where is Craig now?" "No one has really seen him since he quit school but last year rumor had it that he moved across the state line into Arkansas." "Thanks, Tommy, we appreciate your cooperation. You have been a big help." "Yeah, you are welcome, anytime. Just find the SOB that is responsible for this." "Don't worry; we intend to."

Chapter 47

No one was sleeping well on this Saturday night. The detectives are no closer to figuring out what happened to Katrina. Tommy is wondering how someone could commit such an act on such a charming and loving person. Craig is tossing and turning because of the guilt of supplying the Ketamine and for taking the pictures. It didn't matter that he didn't know why he took them. Katrina's parents are lying awake in their bed, blaming themselves for what has happened. Tiffany had a whole different reason for not sleeping. She was at the school using the photo lab developing pictures from her camera. She knew she couldn't drop the camera off at the one hour photo. However, no one was taking it harder than Katrina. She refused to eat. She refused to sleep. She refused to do anything. She sat fully clothed atop her bed, just staring out the window into the darkness. Tears were streaming down her face. She stared into the darkness for hours and then she opened her diary and began to write. *"Dear Diary, Why me? What did I do to deserve this? Why don't I have someone, like a brother or a sister? I just want someone I can confide in or someone I can cry with. I have loving parents but I want more. No, I deserve more. I just want my dreams to come true. Dammit Diary, is that too much to ask?"* She put her diary up and slipped into the shower. While she was in there her cellphone rang. Her voicemail picked up and he left a message. *"Miss Hall this is Tommy. You owe me a dance. As soon as you feel up to it, just let me know. I am giving you*

an extended rain check. After listening to her message she said, "Well maybe not all is lost and maybe, just maybe, my dreams will come true."

Chapter 48

Katrina awoke Sunday morning feeling somewhat refreshed. The effects of the Ketamine were all but gone. However, there was still a gap in her short term memory. She remembered the events leading up to arriving at the dance but the next thing she remembers is waking up in the hospital. She decided against going to church, she really wasn't feeling up to being social. Her parents understood and didn't push the issue. Instead she kept to herself for most of the day. She sat on her bed flipping through her diary, just for the sake of passing the time. She finally got up and took a shower. When she got out, she slipped into her nighty and found her robe. She remembered Tommy's message, and she played it over and over. She had just about psyched herself into calling him back. She did pick up her phone and punch his number into the key pad, but before it had time to ring she hung up. She decided she would see him in the morning. She joined her mother and father for dinner but just picked around on her plate. She asked to be excused. Her parents told her that they were there for her, if she needed them. She hugged them both, cleaned up her dishes and returned to her room. She took off her robe and dropped it onto the floor. Then she said aloud, "Maybe, just maybe, tomorrow will be a better day." She turned out the light and drifted off to sleep.

Chapter 49

Tiffany's parents were out of town on business and her grandmother was fast asleep. She snuck out of her bedroom window, jumped into her car and headed for the school. She still had the keys to the gym entrance. She unlocked the door and headed down the hall towards the school newsletter class. It's where they printed the happenings of the school and it is also where they developed most of the pictures used in the year book. Tiffany spent hours last night developing the pictures Craig had taken. Now she was back to keep her word. She was going to unleash her wrath on Katrina. She printed hundreds of 8x10 photos of Katrina and hung them all over the school. In some she was in her bra and panties and in some she was totally nude. She also printed a few poster sized photos of Craig's "money shot." The caption read: ***"It is true, I am a dirty slut."*** Tiffany looked around and was pleased with her handy work. She ran by the library and hacked into the student files and found the list of cell numbers that some students had provided to the school. She sent out mass texts from a pre-paid cell with photo attachments of a nude Katrina. Tiffany knew the damage was done; know she just had to cover her tracks. She cleaned up all the evidence that would link her to this horrible act of exploitation. She locked up the classroom and dropped the keys to the gym into the lock box. She told her cheer coach that she done that after the dance Friday night. She exited the gym the same way she had entered. Before leaving she made sure the doors locked behind her. She rushed home and crawled back into her house, thru her bedroom window.

She slipped into her bed clothes, went into the kitchen and purposely dropped a glass. Her grandmother jumped up and ran into the kitchen to see what happened. Tiffany explained to her she wasn't feeling well and needed something to drink. Truth was she felt fine. She wanted her grandmother to be her alibi in case she was accused of something. She planned out each and every detail, including, skipping school the morning. As bad as she wanted to see the look on Katrina's face, she knew the humiliation that she would suffer, would last a lifetime.

Chapter 50

The next morning Katrina woke early enough, to put on make-up and fix her hair. She actually got dressed and made it to the kitchen, in time, to sit down and eat a bowl of oatmeal and a slice of buttered toast. After she finished eating, she fixed another small glass of orange juice. She was bound and determined to make this a good day. When she pulled into the school parking lot it was unusually crowded. She saw several students looking at their phones and gawking. She saw some students talking to each other and laughing hysterically. When she got out of her car and started toward the entrance of the school, she saw even more students looking at their phones and then looking at her pointing. Once she entered the school she saw why everyone was in such awe. She didn't realize at first, that the pictures were of her until she saw the one of her face and read the words, ***"I am a dirty slut."*** She turned around with tears in her eyes and saw Tommy walking into the school. She ran right past him, and busted through the double door. She ran to her car and squealed out of the lot. The tears continued flowing down her cheeks. She sped home as fast as she could. Katrina decided that instead of this being a good day, it was going to be the last day of her life. She pulled into her driveway and jumped out of her car. She never even shut the engine off as she ran into the house and to her room. She pulled her diary out from under her bed and began ripping out pages and throwing them all over her room. She ran to her daddy's room and got his gun. After returning to her room, Katrina sat on the end of her bed and placed the gun in her mouth and pulled the trigger. She heard the gun click so she checked the drum and it was empty. She threw the gun onto the floor and ran to the garage and got a rope. She stopped by the kitchen and grabbed a bar stool. After tying the rope to her ceiling fan, she tied the other end into a noose. She slipped the noose around her neck. She climbed up onto the stool and began thinking about her life and where she went wrong. Katrina prayed to God to give her parents strength to deal with her untimely departure. She began rocking the stool back and forth and it, finally, slipped out from underneath her feet. The rope tightened around her throat and she felt the air leaving her body. She saw her life flash before her eyes and instead of seeing the light at the end of the tunnel; she drifted into total darkness. His car came to a screeching halt in front of her house. He jumped out and ran passed her still running car. The door was standing wide open and he immediately imagined the worst. He entered her house blindly not knowing what to expect. He ran from room to room calling her name and he finally caught a glimpse of her lifeless body hanging from the ceiling fan. Tommy had watched enough medical shows, on television, to know that if someone hangs themselves there is usually going to be neck or esophagus injuries. So instead of cutting her down, he quickly placed the stool back under Katrina's feet thus relieving the tension the rope had around her throat. He stood on her bed and untied the rope from the ceiling fan while simultaneously allowing her to lean against him. Once free from the ceiling fan he held her head as still as he could as he laid her onto the floor. She wasn't breathing, however, her body was still warm and she still had fairly good color. He dialed 911 and put his phone on speaker. He followed the operator's instructions and began CPR. He done it for what seemed like hours but in actuality it had only been minutes. He was becoming increasingly exhausted but then he heard sirens wailing in the distance. Knowing that help was on the way he mustered up enough strength to continue. When paramedics arrived on scene Tommy was still trying to revive her. They hurriedly looked her over. They found a slight pulse. Her blood pressure was extremely low, she had visual rope marks on her neck and due to life saving efforts she suffered a few broken ribs. Other than that, the extents of her injuries were unknown. They hurriedly placed her body onto the gurney and whisked her away. Tommy just sat in her floor, in shock, over what had just happened. He finally got up and started out of her room, when he noticed a .38 caliber revolver, lying in the corner of the room. He picked it up and looked it over. He headed out of her room and towards the front door. Just as he began to lay the gun onto the coffee table he heard an officer say, "Drop the gun son and put your hands up." He complied. The moment he dropped it, the officers took him into custody. They didn't read him his rights or place him under arrest; they simply wanted to hear his side of the story. They wanted to know, just what the hell happened here and why he was in Katrina's house.

Part Nine: Confessions

Chapter 51

He walked through the front door and dropped his books on the end table. He grabbed the remote to the television and pushed the "on" button and then it was off to the kitchen. He always came home from school hungry. When he entered the kitchen he found a big surprise. His moms' afternoon surgery had been temporarily postponed due to a glitch in her patients' insurance coverage, so she came home and decided to cook him his favorite meal, homemade Mexican enchiladas. "Hi mom, he boasted cheerfully. You are home early, is something wrong?" "No son, nothing is wrong. I am on call, so I may have to leave at any given moment." "Oh okay. Well, I am starving, I think I am going to grab a snack." "Okay, just don't ruin your appetite. "I won't mom, it looks amazing." Jeffrey poured himself a bowl of Honey nut Cheerios and headed back to the living room to watch the documentary titled: <u>Life in Texas.</u> Just as he began to sit down a message came across the screen that said, "Breaking News out of Nashville Tennessee." Jeffrey stood there with his eyes glued to the television. Finally, a news reporter appeared on screen and began speaking. "We interrupt your regularly scheduled programming to bring you this breaking news story. A Tennessee teenager, Katrina Hall, tried to commit suicide today after falling victim to an apparent sexting scheme. Reports say days after the teen was slipped a date rate drug, pictures of her were leaked to the internet and sent to several students. The perpetrator did not stop there. He or she then proceeded to blow the pictures up and place them in the halls of the school, for everyone to see. This proved to be more than the teen could handle and she tried to end her life by hanging herself. If you have any knowledge about this case authorities are asking you to contact your local police department, FBI, or Crime-stoppers Unit." Before returning to regular scheduled programming, the television station ran a quick recap without sound. It said "Nashville teen listed in critical condition more to come as this story develops," and then a picture appeared on screen. Jeffrey immediately gasped and turned white, as if he had just seen a ghost. His cereal bowl slipped from his hands and came crashing down through the glass coffee table. His mother came running into the living room to see what had happened. She found her son standing there, trembling and pointing at the TV. "Jeffrey, what is it?" He hit the rewind on the DVR remote and then he said, "Look mom, it's the girl, the girl in the mirror." They were both standing there looking at the picture on the television set. It was a picture of a female, whose face looked identical to Jeffrey's, only this female was seven hundred miles away.

Chapter 52

Elizabeth had just gotten out of the bath and decided she needed something to eat. It seemed like she could never get full now that she was eating for two. Nate was asleep on the couch, when she finally made it to the living room. She woke him up trying to pry the remote out of his clasped hand. He got up and kissed her on the forehead and asked her if she was coming to bed. She replied, "yes, but I want to catch the breaking news everyone has been talking about all day. It is coming on in about fifteen minutes." "Okay babe, hurry up. I will keep the bed warm for you," He replied. She sat there watching the last few minutes of an unknown sitcom. Just as expected, the local news started out with new information surrounding the earlier breaking story. She turned up a can of Pepsi and took a drink just as the news anchor said, "Earlier this afternoon we told you that a Nashville teen identified as Katrina Hall tried committing suicide today. After hearing those words, Elizabeth spit out the soda she had in her mouth and yelled for Nate. He came running and asked, "What is it E, is it the baby?" "No, watch this." They both watched and couldn't believe what they were seeing. Someone Elizabeth watched grow from a newborn infant into a strikingly beautiful young woman had just tried taking her own life. It was heartbreaking to say the least. She grabbed ahold of a shirtless Nate and hugged him and quietly sobbed. He sat there doing his best to comfort her. Her mind drifted back to the first day she took over as the twins' case worker. She was handed two envelopes that were labeled John and Jane Doe. She opened the envelopes and found that each one contained the same things. Knowing that this was a closed adoption, Elizabeth knew that she had to wait until the kids were eighteen and of legal age before giving them the envelopes, that were left to them by their biological mother or she could lose her job. She put the envelopes into a lock box and forgot about them, for all these years. After seeing that Katrina or "Jane Doe" tried killing herself, she thought the hell with her job and this closed adoption. She was on the verge of taking a maternity leave anyway. She told Nate that she was going to contact the Jacks' first thing in the morning and let them know the entire, unedited truth, surrounding the adoption of the Coleman twins. Then she would fly to Nashville and check up on the Hall's and fill them in as well. He questioned her about Mac and Bobby and the only thing she could say was, "Shit, Mac!" "What is it, Nate asked?" "Oh my God, Nate, Mac knows he has a granddaughter named Katrina. He is a smart man so how long before he figures out that it's her. I have to include him in on this." "And Bobby, Nate asked?" "My first instinct is screw him, Bobby has been a constant thorn in my side but I am tired of carrying the secret of the twins' identities around with me and I have to do what is best for me and my unborn child. So yes he has to be included also. Nate called Bobby and Elizabeth called Mac. They would meet with the both of them before meeting with the Jacks'. Even though everything would come to a head sooner than expected, Elizabeth was not ready for a face to face reunion of biological father and son and she wasn't sure Jeffrey was ready for that either.

Chapter 53

The next morning Nate and Elizabeth drove to the restaurant simply called the Diner. It served the best fried eggs and peppered bacon. Elizabeth was starving. Nate teased her when she placed her order, jokingly saying that she was going to wind up as big as a house if she kept eating like that. The waitress looked at him with a hard look and then Nate said, "What, it was a joke, she is eating for two." The waitress then smiled and sort of giggled. As they were waiting for their food to arrive, Mac showed up. Just minutes later, Bobby came in as well. Mac said, "What the hell is he doing here?" "I could ask the same thing about you, Bobby replied." Elizabeth spoke with a quiet but stern voice, "Bobby sit down and shut up. I have news to share with both of you and it could be a matter of life and death." They both looked at her and neither said another word. Her breakfast arrived. The waitress sat three plates in front of her. She told Nate his would be right out. Elizabeth had ordered three eggs over easy, bacon, buttered toast, gravy and biscuits, two waffles with strawberries and cool whip and a side of hash browns. Bobby kept his mouth shut until Elizabeth had almost eaten everything on all three plates. "Did you bring me all the way down here to watch you eat?" "No smart ass. I was making sure you both could sit beside each other for more than five minutes because what I am fixing to tell you is going to change many lives. Not just for a little while but forever." After the waitress cleared the table they all four ordered coffee. "Once I begin, I don't want any interruptions or questions. I simply want you both to listen and then I want you both to take the information home and process it. I must ask you both not to repeat anything I tell you until all parties involved have been talked to. Do we have a deal?" Mac immediately said, "Deal." This was not the first time Elizabeth and Mac had a heart to heart. Bobby finally spoke up and said, "Deal." Elizabeth wasn't stupid. She told him if he broke his word the police would find out that he was involved in the break in at her office. Elizabeth cut right to the chase. She began by telling them that a girl named Katrina from Tennessee had been drugged and photographed nude. Despite being asked not to interrupt or ask questions, Bobby couldn't help himself. "Why tell us this? We don't even know her. Mac sat up in his chair and quickly glanced across the table at her. He spoke up and said, "Elizabeth, he is right, why now? What does this have to do with us?" She cleared her throat and took a drink of her Luke warm coffee. "I chose now…" She paused for a brief moment as tears began to trickle down her face. Nate took her hand and told her to continue. "I chose now because it's all over the news." "What is?" Bobby interrupted again. "Mac the girl who tried unsuccessfully to hang herself is your granddaughter, Katrina Hall." Mac fell back into his seat, "Oh dear God, her parents must be torn all to pieces." "Screw them Mac, she needs to see us and she needs to know who we are," Bobby said. "Don't jump the gun Bobby, she won't be seeing or talking to anyone for a while, doctor's orders." "I am going to see one of my other clients in just a few minutes so go home and wait by the phones. If all goes well and they agree to it, you can accompany me and Katrina's "brother" to Nashville." They all left the Diner and went their separate ways. Elizabeth arrived at her office fifteen minutes before she expected the Jacks'. She heard a bubbly voice behind her say, "Hello Miss Evan's I was not expecting you." "I know Jill; I called a special meeting today with one of my clients. I need you to make sure the conference room across from my office stays un-booked for at least the next half hour." "Yes ma'am. I will do." "Oh and Jill please, under no circumstances, let anyone disturb us." Elizabeth unlocked the lock box that was under her desk and retrieved the packages addressed to John and Jane Doe, and headed to the conference room. She had just gotten things laid out when she heard a knock on the door. Jill stuck her head in and announced the arrival of the Jacks' and the proceeded to usher them in.

Chapter 54

Once the door closed behind them, Elizabeth thanked them for coming on short notice. "Richard and Marianne, I have asked you down here today to let you in on the details surrounding Jeffrey's adoption seventeen years ago. After I finish I hope you understand things a little better. Jeffrey, I think you will find that the doctors not only misdiagnosed you for a second time but that there is a perfectly scientific and spiritual reason for you seeing the "girl in the mirror." So let me just start from the beginning." Almost eighteen years ago a scared pregnant young teenager by the name of Melanie Anne Coleman came into our office and told us she wished to give her children up for adoption. She wanted it to be a closed adoption. This meant neither family would get to meet the other. Month after month she would come here after her doctor visits and she would tell us of the babies' progress. She fell in the high risk category so she had to have multiple ultrasounds. Every ultrasound she had, showed the twins touching each other. Once they even got a shot where it looked as if they were communicating with one another. The male twin was even captured patting the female on the head as if consoling her. Doctors say the wonders surrounding child birth are so profound that there could really be a strong spiritual bond between twins even while they are still in the womb. Anyways, she called me the day of her eight month visit and told me her dad told her he was going to meet her after the appointment and they were going to go get something to eat. She didn't argue because she was going to tell her dad that she had had a change of heart. She wanted to keep her twins. At her appointment, however, she was told they were going to have to induce labor because of preeclampsia. She called her dad and told him and he told her not to worry that he would meet her at home and he would drive her back to the hospital because of the fast approaching storm. She sat out on her way home when an eighteen wheeler forced her off the road into in coming traffic. She hit another vehicle head on. After being taken to the hospital, doctors quickly delivered the twins but Melanie died from unforeseen complications, before making a formal declaration stating she no longer chose to give her babies up. There wasn't a dry eye in the room. Richard said, "That is a touching story but what does that have to do with us?" "Well, you see, Jeffrey is the male twin and Katrina Hall, his "girl in the mirror" is the female twin of whom I speak. Melanie was their mother. She was scared to death when she found out they were going to induce labor so she prayed to God that no matter what happened that the twins always stay connected somehow. I think she got her wish. Katrina wrote often in her diary about the repetitive dreams she had, where she would run and play with her brother. I have a package for you Jeffrey and then I need to ask something from you all. She hands Jeffrey the package and tells him that the contents are from his biological mother and to only open it when he feels it's the right time. Then she turns her attention to his parents. "I realize you too are both surgeons and can't just leave without notice but I would like for Jeffrey to accompany me to Tennessee, to see Katrina in person and hopefully be able to offer her some kind of comfort. I realize this is a lot to swallow but please go home and consider it and let me know what you decide. I'm sorry for not telling you all this sooner."

Chapter 55

On the way home, Mr. and Mrs. Jacks were very quiet, neither one of them said so much as a word. Jeffrey couldn't take it anymore, so he broke the silence. "Mom, Dad, this doesn't change anything. Y'all are still my parents. The only parents, I have ever known. I will always be your son." "We know that you feel that way now Jeffrey but what happens when you meet your real father?" "You are my real father. You taught me how to throw a curve ball, you taught me how to swing a bat, and ride a bike. Dad it takes more than blood and DNA to make someone a father. Mom, that goes for you as well. You taught me how to wash my clothes, clean my room, and how to make chocolate gravy. Y'all are my parents and always will be. Do I want to meet my other blood relatives? Yes, I guess I do. Do I feel I need to go visit Katrina in the hospital? Yes, I think I should. So mom, can you talk to the school and get me excused for a week or so? I have enough credits to graduate already, I am just taking classes to be taking them." "Son, if this is really what you feel in your heart that you need to do; your father and I will not stand in your way. Besides, you are practically an adult and I think it's time you started making adult decisions. So, yes you may go with Elizabeth on her trip to Tennessee. I will call the school, first thing, Monday morning,"

Chapter 56

Elizabeth and Nate made reservations for the earliest flight possible leaving out on Monday morning. After all other arrangements for their trip were finalized; Elizabeth breathed a sigh of relief. She couldn't believe what kind of day she had already had and it was just passed noon. She had talked to Mac and Bobby, she had a conference room visit with the Jacks' and she had quit her job all within about five hours. On the other hand, she did feel some sort of accomplishment. She put on a jogging suit, put her hair up into her signature, braided ponytail, grabbed her keys and kissed Nate passionately on the lips. He asked, "Where do you think you are going, Miss Evans?" "I want to jump in my mustang with the top down, turn the radio up and just drive for a bit. I just want to clear my mind a little." "Do you want company?" "Actually, this is something I want to do on my own, if you don't mind" Elizabeth drove around for hours just enjoying the slight breeze and singing along to the radio. It was playing an all day tribute to the Eighties and Nineties. Then it hit her like a slap in the face. She knew in her heart of hearts exactly where she needed to be.

Chapter 57

When she pulled up at the cemetery, her stomach felt as if it were in a thousand knots. She made her way down that concrete walkway and as she approached the big old oak tree she could see the silhouette of a man, knelt down at Melanie's grave. Once she reached her destination, she realized that the man was Bobby. "What are you doing here, Miss Evans?" Well, I was just driving around trying to clear my mind and it hit me. I needed to talk to Melanie, just to make sure that what I am planning on doing is the right thing to do." "I guess you could say that's why I am here. When I left the Diner this morning I started feeling guilty about everything I have done. Then I realized just how selfish I have been. I didn't give a damn about anyone else but myself. So, I decided to come visit her as well. Look Miss Evans, I am sorry about everything. I am not going to go to Tennessee with you. Instead I am going to do the right thing. Something I should have done months ago. I am going to answer for all my wrong doings. Don't worry; I will not mention you or Nate. Goodbye Miss Evans, I hope you find the answers you seek. As for me, I hope I can get all these legal issues put behind me." "Good luck Bobby. I hope you do to. I don't think you are a bad person, you have just made a few bad decisions." "Thanks that means a lot, especially coming from you Miss Evans." Elizabeth sat there under that tree for a little while longer, wondering if she was making the right decision, by allowing Jeffrey to see Katrina. Her cell phone began ringing so she looked at the caller ID, and realized that she had, because the caller on the other end of the phone was Jeffrey.

Chapter 58

Elizabeth made the journey back towards the house. This time however, she had the top up. The sun was beginning to set and the air was cool and crisp. She tried calling Nate but he didn't answer his phone. She wasn't worried about him because she figured he was passed out on the couch with the remote in his hand. Well, there was no reason for her to worry but he wasn't asleep. He was purposely avoiding her call. He knew she was just calling to say that she was on the way home and he wanted to surprise her. He had cooked up a delicious looking pan of Chicken Alfredo and homemade, Italian dinner rolls. When Elizabeth walked through the door she couldn't help but smile. She found Nate standing in the kitchen over a freshly chopped bowl of chef salad. He looked up and said, "Hello my lady, welcome to Nate's Kitchen." They both chuckled. He said, "I hope you are hungry." She replied, "Me and the baby on board are famished." After dinner the duo went over just how things should go once they landed in Tennessee. She filled him in on her conversation with Bobby and her phone call from Jeffrey then they decided to call it a night. They crawled into bed and she laid her head on his shoulder. After a moment she looked up at him and said, "Please tell me this is all going to end well." He replied, "I don't know how it will end but trust me, you have done and are doing everything you can to make sure it will."

Chapter 59

The lovebirds were up and ready to go before the alarm even went off. Neither one could sleep. Elizabeth just tossed and turned and Nate woke with every movement. They went over the plan once more before leaving the house. "Okay, Mac will be arriving around twelve to thirteen hours after us, since he decided to drive. He will meet us at the hotel. Honey, I am counting on you not only to introduce Jeffrey and Mac but to keep them out of site until I get done talking to the Hall's." "I know, stop worrying, it is going to be okay." "Well let's get going. We have to stop by and pick up Jeffrey and we don't want to miss our flight." "He reached around her from the back and rubbed the sides of her growing baby bump. Then he said, "Are you sure it is safe for a pregnant woman to fly?" "Shut up," she said jokingly. She turned around and as she looked into his baby blues, he took her face into his hands and gently leaned in and planted the softest kiss upon her lips. They grabbed their bags and headed out the door.

Chapter 60

Their plane left Austin-Bergstrom International Airport at Eight a.m. sharp. Once in the air nerves really began to set in. Elizabeth knew now without a shadow of a doubt, there was no turning back. She had come too far and had gotten too many people involved, not to see this thing through. She put in her IPod headphones. She heard John Mayer, singing into her ears. Her head hit the pillow and just as fast as she drifted off, she was awakened by Nate. "Wake up babe. We are fixing to land at Nashville International. You had better buckle up." "Man, that was a quick flight," she said. The plane landed and as they were exiting the plane the pilot was reminding everyone to reset their watches. They had left one time zone and landed in another. It was almost eleven a.m. so the trio jumped into the rental car that was waiting on them and headed out in search of a place to eat and a place to sleep.

Chapter 61

Mac drove for about seven hours straight and was just a little over half way there. He wasn't a spring chicken anymore and he was beginning to ache all over. He decided to find a place to stop for a while. Once he got settled in, he called Elizabeth. "Hey Elizabeth, it's me. I drove until I couldn't drive anymore. I found a cheap hotel about six hours this side of Nashville's city limits. I'm going to rest a few hours and about nightfall, I will resume driving. What hotel did you all find?" "We are at the Doubletree Suites, located on Fourth Ave. Be careful Mac." "Always have and always will," He replied.

Chapter 62

"What's wrong with Mac," Nate asked in a hushed voice?" "Nothing, he is just tired that's all. He said he was still about six hours out. Since he isn't going to get here until after visiting hours tonight, I think I'm going to go to the hospital and get an update on Katrina and fill the Hall's in on all of our arrivals. Why don't you and Jeffrey order room service and catch a game or something. "Sounds like a plan. Hey Jeffrey, do you want to order pizza and catch a game on T.V.?" "Sure, sounds fun. Can I call my parents first and let them know we made it to the hotel?" "Of course, you are an adult and you don't need our permission." "Thanks Nate, I will be right back and we will catch that game." "He is a great kid Elizabeth. We can hold down the fort here. Go see the Hall's." She kissed him, grabbed her keys to the rental car and headed to the hospital.

Chapter 63

Once at the hospital, she began her search for the Martin and Renee. She stopped by the patient help desk. "Excuse me, I am looking for Katrina Hall's room, can you please help me?" "She isn't being allowed visitors at this time, per her parents' request." "Where might I find her parents?" "They left word that if anyone needed them, they would be in the cafeteria, on the lower level." "Thank you so much." As Elizabeth made her way down to the lower level, she began to let her nerves get the best of her. She really didn't know what to expect from the Hall's. She entered the cafeteria and she spotted them at the same time they seen her. They jumped up and ran up to her. "What's wrong Miss Evans, is it Katrina?" "Yes, but it isn't what you think." "Well if you just wanted to check on her you would have called. So what is it that has brought you all the way here from Texas, Miss Evans?" "Please call me Elizabeth." Your right, I came here for a reason. I want to share with you the details surrounding the adoption of Katrina. There is something you should know. Please just listen and if you still have questions when I am done, I will answer them as best I can." Elizabeth told them the whole story. At first they just sat there silently, as if playing the popular preschool game, quiet mouse still mouse but after a few moments, Mrs. Hall spoke. "So, what you are proposing is that we meet Jeffrey and Mac and then we allow Jeffrey to go in and see our daughter." "Yes, we can show up here in the morning, you can meet them over breakfast and then during morning visitation hours we let Jeffrey go in and introduce himself and hopefully get some kind of response." "Well, what do you think honey?" "I think at this point anything is worth a try. Who knows, Miss Evans might just be on to something. This may give her something worth living for." Elizabeth apologized for dumping the news on them, the way she did and then she excused herself.

Chapter 64

Once back at the hotel, she found both guys fast asleep. She finished watching the last inning of a baseball game and then jumped in the shower. As the warm water hit her head and trickled down her naked flesh she felt a huge burden lifted off of her shoulders. She no longer had to protect the twins from outsiders because she had successfully laid the groundwork to bring them back together. Yes, the twins would be together for the first time since birth. The baby inside her began kicking and it snapped her back to reality. She decided that that was her cue to get out. She turned off the faucet and joined Nate in bed. As her head hit her pillow, she realized that tomorrow was going to be an emotional day for everyone involved.

Chapter 65

Mac's plan of sleeping for a few hours and getting back on the road failed. He overslept. It was two o'clock in the morning when he finally got up and took care of the three S's. Then he loaded his suitcase into the car and headed out. He called Elizabeth after reaching the outskirts of Nashville. She told him not to worry and informed him that she had already talked to the Hall's and explained to him that they agreed to meet him and Jeffrey. She told him to drive straight to the hospital and she would meet him in the parking garage on the first level. Mac parked on level three. He stepped into the elevator and rode it to level one. When the doors opened Mac couldn't believe what he saw. For a split second, he could have sworn that he saw Melanie standing in front of him. After all the introductions were made, they were finally ready to meet up with the Hall's. Elizabeth introduced everyone to the Hall's and they all ordered breakfast. It was a little bit awkward for everyone but especially Jeffrey. He felt like everyone was staring at him and to a point they were. Martin and Renee couldn't get over the fact that he looked so much like their Katrina and Mac couldn't believe how much he looked like his daughter. Finally, Jeffrey spoke. "I know you are my grandfather but by means beyond our control we were separated and I really don't know you so for now I am simply going to call you Mr. Coleman. I want to thank everyone for having faith in me. I hope by me talking to her we get some kind of response." Martin spoke up and said, "Son any response will be better than what we have now." "Okay then,

Elizabeth I am ready to go see my sister." "Okay then let us all go to the waiting room outside of the ICU. After entering the waiting room, Jeffrey proceeded to hit the buzzer. After the double doors swung open he proceeded down the hall. He found the room he was searching for, knocked and proceeded to slip inside. Once he laid his eyes upon her, his heart began beating fast, he broke out into a cold sweat and he felt as if he were going to faint. He was literally staring at the "girl in the mirror," in the flesh, lying so innocently in the hospital bed. She wasn't hooked up to a lot of tubes and wires but she did have an IV, which delivered fluids to keep her hydrated. Her stats were all pretty normal but she wasn't alert. She just laid there staring blankly into the mirror that was hanging on the wall, above the sink. Her reflection was staring back at her. So he knew she could see him in the mirror as well, however, she still didn't move or even blink. He began by introducing himself. "Katrina, I am so sorry. I know you don't know me from Adam but I am your brother. Our birth mother was killed in a tragic, traffic accident and we were given up for adoption and thus separated. I don't know how or why but I could see you from time to time in my reflections. It scared me because I didn't know what was happening. I started seeing a doctor who diagnosed me with a "phobia" of mirrors. The last time I saw your reflection you asked for help and I see now that I let you down. Tears began running down his cheeks as he continued talking. Katrina, I just want to say I am truly sorry from the bottom of my heart. I should have figured out what was going on. I will never leave you again. That is my promise to you." Jeffrey was allowing his emotions to get the best of him, so he thought it would be wise to step out of the room for a few moments to pull himself back together. Before he did, he leaned over and kissed her on the cheek. His tears fell upon her face. He gently brushed across her face to wipe the tears away then he hurriedly headed towards the door, before he lost it. Just as he started out of the room, he heard a soft voice that was barely audible say, "Please don't go; I have dreamed of this very day." He turned back around and she was sitting up in the bed. He walked back to her and took her hand in his. "You are real. I mean, I thought you were just another figment of my imagination." "Yes Katrina, I am real." "I have only seen you in my dreams but here you are. I was determined to lie in this bed and not say another word to anyone. I feel so humiliated." "Katrina there are a lot of people in the waiting room that love you. You can't shut them out. Your parents are out there, so are Elizabeth and Nate and they brought someone with them other than me." "Great a shrink, that's just what I need." "It is not a shrink." "Well who then?" "It's…well I call him Mr. Coleman but he is our grandfather on our mother's side. It seems we have a father and grandparents on his side too, back in Texas." "I have family in Texas?" "Yes, it is a long story but when you get out of here we can talk about all that. Besides, we have packages that are addressed to Baby Jane and John Doe to open. I didn't want to do it alone so I waited on you." "Well now that you are here, I am ready to go home. Please go get my parents and the doctor." "Gladly," He said, as he hugged his sister. Jeffrey went back to the waiting room with a smile on his face. "Mr. and Mrs. Jacks grab a doctor." "Why, what's wrong?" "Nothing ma'am but my sister is awake and she is ready to go home. She said four days in hell is long enough." Everyone giggled as her parent's asked the nurse on call, to page the doctor. The doctor came in and checked her out. It didn't take long to determine that there was no medical reason to keep her any longer. However, he did want her to talk to a family psychiatrist that was on staff, before he discharged her. She agreed to talk with him. Katrina was at the point; she would do anything to go home. Her parent's each hugged her and told her how much they loved her. Mac introduced himself as Mr. Coleman; he didn't want to push himself on her. Elizabeth told her how proud she was of the young woman that she had become. After their reunion came to an end and everyone went back out into the waiting room, Jeffrey slipped back in. He was holding two envelopes. He handed her an enveloped and playfully teased her by saying, "Here you go Baby Jane, I think this belongs to you." While waiting for the psychiatrist, they decided to open their envelopes. Inside they each found a picture of their birth mother and father, an ultra sound photo of the two of them cuddled up to one another and a hand written letter, explaining to them the reason why, she thought it best to give them up. She told them in the letter that she loved them and hoped they found each other if ever they became separated. They were both very emotional. They hugged each other and then he helped her over to the sink, so she could clean up a bit and at least brush her teeth. He stood there beside her in case she needed support, because she had been off her feet for days. She washed her face and brushed her teeth and then she laid her head onto his shoulder. As they were standing there looking at their reflections in the mirror, they noticed the room grow cold. They started towards the bed but then both froze and turned back towards the mirror. This time though, the reflection looking back at them wasn't theirs, it was that of a seventeen year old girl. It was their mother. She spoke, "I prayed to God, that my children would always be together. Remember, as long as the Sun rises in the morning and the moon and stars light up the night skies I will always be watching over you from Heaven. After those words, the reflection disappeared and the room immediately warmed back up. There was a knock on the door. They were both expecting the psychiatrist, but to their surprise in walked Bobby.

Epilogue: Revelations

Once Katrina had her psychiatric evaluation, her doctor signed her discharge papers. Jeffrey's parents decided to fly up unexpectedly. They were going nuts not having him in Texas. Once everyone met up outside, they decided to go grab something to eat. Katrina didn't care where they chose to go; she was as hungry as a horse. After they ate, all of them exchanged numbers and addresses and promised to stay in touch. Bobby explained to Elizabeth that he turned himself in and after agreeing to testify against Slim, he was cut a break. "The judged ordered me to two years unsupervised probation. Authorities found Slim in a Seven Eleven bathroom, however he was deceased. He died from an apparent overdose. The needle was still stuck in his arm. He also had in his possession a bloody bat. Authorities in Texas and Tennessee believe it was the bat I took to the back of the head but they doubt Slim had it in his possession at the time of the incident." Elizabeth found Nate and they hugged the twins and said their goodbyes. They drove to the airport and hopped on the next flight to home sweet home. Bobby hugged his kids and told them that he was glad he had finally found them and that he hoped he could be a part of their lives in the future. He said his last goodbyes. They promised that they would stay in contact with him. Bobby tearfully got into his car and sped away. He had to get back to his hotel. Mac told his grandkids that it meant the world to him, to have met them. They responded by telling him that grandpa would hear from them often. He grinned as he walked away. He turned around once more as he was headed to his car. He saw his daughter in the both of them. They were holding hands and waving at him with the others. The kids' parents were talking the whole time and they reached the same conclusion. They came to the realization that these two were going to be inseparable. So the Hall's decided to sell their house and move back to Texas. Martin would get his old job back as a truck driver and that is exactly what they did. Katrina finished her senior year at home and then enrolled at the University of Texas where she began studying Investigative Reporting and Business Law. Jeffrey graduated with honors. He also enrolled at the University of Texas, where he began studying Business Management. Bobby told him the hotel was his as soon as he got his degree. Craig got word Tommy was being questioned about the whole Katrina fiasco and he began to feel guilty. He felt it necessary to set the story straight. After all, he didn't want Tommy to find out that he had had an encounter with his brother while on the lacrosse team, so Craig took the tape recorder to the police and turned himself in. After police listened to the recording, they got a warrant for Tiffany and her camera. Craig agreed to testify on behalf of the prosecution in exchange for a suspended sentence and two and a half years of probation. Tiffany was convicted and sentenced to one year in a minimum security all girls prison, five years of probation and two hundred and forty hours of community service. She also lost her cheer scholarship. Tommy got a four year football scholarship to none other than the University of Texas. Perhaps, somewhere along the way, he will run into a girl named Katrina, who owes him a dance. Elizabeth and Nate finally got around to making wedding plans and knew they had to do it soon. The twins agreed to be the best man and matron of honor. Bobby recommended his dad perform the ceremony. The invitations were sent and everything was set. Two weeks later it was show time. Everyone showed up including the Jacks', the Hall's, The Ellis's, Bobby, Jill, Mac, Jerry, Mary, and Melanie's best friend Tamara. Mac filled her in on the crazy situation and invited her to come see her once best friend's kids. The wedding went off without a hitch... Well, almost. Just as Pastor Ellis was about to announce them husband and wife, Elizabeth stopped him. Everyone gasped. Nate said, "What's wrong honey?" Elizabeth looked back to the pastor and asked, "We are legally married right now, aren't we?" He replied, "Yes." She then replied, "Good because my water just broke, Emma Grace McKinley is on the way." She grabbed Nate by the arm and they ran to her Mustang GT.

To be continued...

Would you like to see your manuscript become a book?

If you are interested in becoming a PublishAmerica author, please submit your manuscript for possible publication to us at:

mybook@publishamerica.com

You may also mail in your manuscript to:

**PublishAmerica
PO Box 151
Frederick, MD 21705**

www.publishamerica.com

PublishAmerica